ISBN: 0-930625-67-6
Library of Congress Catalog Card Number: 97-72121

Editor: *Allan Miller*
Editorial Assistant: *Elizabeth Stephan*
Designer: *Darryl Keck*
Cover Design: *Jaro Sebek*

Cover photo credits:

Front cover: *Top row (left to right)*—Five-inch Dam Troll, courtesy of Lisa Schelitzche; Chatty Cathy, courtesy of Paula Carranza; Platinum Blonde Swirl with White Lipstick Barbie, courtesy of Trisha Nerney; Alice in Wonderland Terri Lee, courtesy of Sandy Dorsey.

Bottom row (left to right)—Helen Blue "Courtney Erin" Cabbage Patch, courtesy of Vicki Tuttell; Carrot Top Pepper, courtesy of Linda Ladd; Side-part Betsy McCall, courtesy of Tina Ritari; Jimmy Cowboy, courtesy of Shari Ogilvie.

Back cover: 36-inch Shirley Temple, courtesy of John Sonnier.

Printed in the United States of America

To order additional copies of this
book or a catalog please contact:

Antique Trader Books
P.O. Box 1050
Dubuque, Iowa 52004
1-800-334-7165

Antique Trader Books
A division of Landmark Specialty Publications

TABLE OF CONTENTS

Acknowledgments iv

Introduction v

Restoring Your Rarities vii

1) Barbie Rarities 1

2) Francie Rarities 20

3) Skipper Rarities 23

4) Chatty Cathy Rarities 27

5) Liddle Kiddles Rarities 42

6) Terri Lee Rarities 59

7) Ginnette Rarities 71

8) Jill Rarities 76

9) Cabbage Patch Rarities 80

10) Tammy Rarities 90

11) Sasha Rarities 106

12) Alexanderkin Rarities 111

13) Mattel Rarities 114

14) Troll Rarities 121

15) Dawn Rarities 135

16) Effanbee Rarities 140

17) Jem Rarities 143

18) Horsman Rarities 148

19) Doll Buggy Rarities 151

20) Paper Doll Rarities 155

21) Other Rarities 177
(Penny Brite, Suzy Cute, Ginny, Tinny Tears, Betsy
McCall, Martha Thompson, Little Marcy, Mrs. Revlon,
Crissy, Eloise, Tressy, Linda Williams, Lustre Creme,
Celluloid, Original Boxes, Store Displays)

Index 196

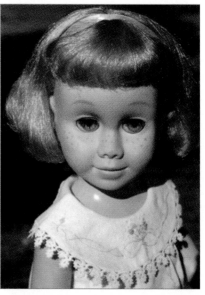

ACKNOWLEDGEMENTS

This *book would not have been possible without
the help of these "Living Dolls"*

Lynn Artel

Jeanne Beaumot

Donna Braun

Sally Broome

Katherine Burrows

Steven Carissimo

Paula Carranza

Terry Carter

Rick Conlon

Patti Cooke

Joy Crawford

Sandy Dorsey

Lawahna Eldred

Grace Frowd

Melody Gocher

Christine Gunderson

Beth Gunther

Kent Gunther

Dieter Jeschke

Ruth Kibbons

Lynn Barringer Krebs

Eugenia Kurz

Linda Ladd

The J. Lawrence Collection

Marty Liston

Jackie Litchfield

Sue Munsell

Trisha Nerney

Shari Ogilvie

Pat Rather

Dorene Reed

Tina Ritari

Jill Salerno

Lynn Schelitzche

Mark and Lisa Scherzer

Rhonda Schoenick

Patricia Snyder

John Sonnier

Linda Strumski

Vicki Tuttell

Tara Wood

INTRODUCTION

The way I see it, doll collecting is a passion that builds slowly but surely over a period of years. Its seeds are planted, no doubt, in childhood, when some angel-faced package made her appearance, first under the Christmas tree, and later by our side in the sandbox or maybe the bath tub, then being wheeled about the neighborhood in her own stroller—making us proud and happy, sharing our chicken pox and our secret code words, and keeping us company as only she could. Then, as her place in our heart was slowly replaced by rock stars and lip gloss, she finds her way up to some shelf, collecting dust and quietly peering at our life from a distance, no longer a real part of it.

Next, she's packed in a box, as we are packed up for college, and after degrees, long 9 to 5 days, marriage and children, we suddenly spot her exact clone sitting on a table at an antique mall (Oh, God, am I old enough to have my childhood toys classified as antiques?) Your eyes lock and nostalgia starts tapping at your shoulder. THIS is where it starts! You take her home, clean her up, and place her in a special spot— perhaps a cabinet. Three years later, she's hard to find, crowded in by the 300 or so other beauties you have since acquired at antique malls, specialty shops, doll shows, flea markets and from collector's ad papers.

For so many of the collectors I talk to, "Doll Hunts" are a regular and invigorating part of their lives. First, you're delighted to find a Franci in the $2.00 box at a flea market, or an old Ginny dress at a neighborhood garage sale. Soon, you're setting your alarm for 6 a.m. to be the very first at ALL the neighborhood garage sales, with the classifieds in one hand and a clever little map you drew-up in the other—just to save time. I

have a theory that when the cave men had their garage sales, prehistoric doll collectors were always the first ones to arrive—prompt, but never pushy, y'know?

But within the realm of doll collecting, NOTHING is more satisfying and rewarding than uncovering a rarity—that un-thought-of hair color variation, the fascinating green eyes on an always blue-eyed doll, the "thought to be just a rumor" accessory purse, those original store displays that are at such a premium, or that one particular item that is one of a scattering that were ever made in the first place.

Where did these rare items come from? There are several explanations . . .

Store displays and limited issues are hard to find for an obvious reason—very few were ever made to begin with. Special promotional items such as posters were never available to the general public, making them especially enticing to the advanced collector.

But other rarities that exist on the secondary doll market aren't as easily explained. Why a certain, rather common tagged outfit will suddenly turn up in a different color is a puzzle to all of us. Foreign knock-offs are a possible explanation for color or print variations in outfits that are not tagged. Chatty Cathy, for example, had a few of her dresses replicated by companies other than Mattel (her manufacturer). There are slight variations that only a knowledgeable Chatty Cathy collector could pick up on, such as slightly wider stripes on the Pink Peppermint Stick dress, or a different style of snap closure. When these variations are found without the official "Chatty Cathy" tag, they are thought to fall in the "Foreign Knock Off" category. When other variations, however, are found tagged, the best any of us can do is conjecture.

Some rarities are the result of factory flukes. Former workers on various production lines have admitted to occasionally inserting, for example, brown eyes into a normally blue-eyed doll, just to break-up the monotony. Little could they have realized that they were creating a future sought-after rarity that would eventually bring as much as $700—the cost at the time of four semesters of college tuition.

In the case of Mattel, where so many variations exist, these unusual quirks are often thought to be the result of simple frugality. Mattel reportedly used every last doll part at the end of a production run, whether it matched or not. Thank you, Mattel, for inadvertently adding such interest and intrigue to our collecting!

The story of the side-part American Girl Barbie doll is an interesting one in the realm of variations. In the mid-1960s Mattel issued Barbie with a new hair-do—a straight, middle part with bangs, about chin length. What most people refer to as a "pageboy" has come to be known as an "American Girl" style in Barbie terms. This simple, ultra-casual style looked great with the corresponding Barbie fashions of the time, with the exception of evening wear. The unpretentious pageboy was just too plain to properly show off prom dresses, evening gowns, etc. The simple addition of a side part added a more sophisticated, bouffant look to the dolls' hair. A few of these side parts were reportedly made up for photographic purposes to model the Barbie evening wear of the time. Because these are so rare, and because the side part actually created a more beautiful doll, they are huge favorites with collectors. The majority of these side parts seem to be from the New York State area.

Certain items, such as the Talking Terri Lee doll, are incredibly hard to find anywhere in the country, except for the state of California. (There are many variations that show up largely in California, where Mattel had its base. Except for the New York side-part connection, I have not found another vatiation-state tie-in.)

Throw-away items such as boxes and original packaging, paper dolls, wrist tags, etc. are pricey today because the great majority of these materials were, of course, disposed of. Any collector today, with an entire room in the basement devoted to doll boxes alone, will tell you that this is no longer the case. Collectors, as well as the average consumer, have come to acknowledge the future value of original packaging and are holding on to it by the reams. Ironically, this realization is, of course, diminishing the value of these doll boxes, etc., as the more these items are conserved, the less they are valued. (Please refer—"Supply and Demand" lecture—9th grade—Sister Marie Barbara.)

Most of the items in the book are not priced, because they couldn't be, responsibly. Too often price guides are written with no tie-in to reality. When items are considered rare, there are simply not enough of them to accurately arrive at a dollar worth. If you uncover one of these rare items in your collection or in your mother's attic, and it is not priced in this book, the best method for selling it is to collect bids from a number of collectors who collect within the line that the doll is in.

I hope that I have explained what a rarity is and I hope you all have the pleasure, at some point, of uncovering one. You may already have one of the items in this book. You may have already sold one of the items seen in this book for a quarter or half-dollar. Either way, this book will help both collectors and dealers alike to siphon out and identify the rare items in all of the major doll lines! Remember the analogy section of those standardized IQ tests? If you do, perhaps this will help to clarify further:

Rarity is to Doll Collecting
as Hope Diamond is to Cubic Zirconia
and Sunshine is to Summer
and Needle is to Haystack.... Good Luck

RESTORING YOUR RARITIES

The chances of finding a mint, pristine rarity at an area flea market are slim. If you do discover one of these rarities, she may be offered by a dealer in the know at top dollar, or she may be a garage sale orphan, in need of some tender loving care to restore her to her former status. The following are some basic cleaning tips for modern vinyl dolls.

RESTORING VINYL

Many collectors have had wonderful luck using Soft Scrub on vinyl limbs, adding a toothbrush for the tougher dirt. THIS METHOD IS NEVER TO BE USED ON OR AROUND FACE PAINT OR BY THE GRILL WORK AROUND VOICE BOXES. For these areas, a simple diaper wipe will work wonders!

Tarn X can be used to remove the green that appears around Barbie ears. This discoloration is caused by a reaction of the metal earring posts with the doll's vinyl. If the doll has red lips, DO NOT submerge the head in Tarn X—use moistened cotton balls inside and outside of the green area and check frequently. Collectors have also had wonderful luck with "Remov-zit".

For ink or marker stains on vinyl—Oxy 5, Clearasil Vanishing Formula and Vicks VapoRub, combined with a little direct sunlight, have all been very helpful. Several applications may be needed for more stubborn marks.

For general repainting of faded lips, eyebrows, etc., Terry Carter of Toney, Alabama, an avid doll collector, suggests LIQUITEX brand craft paint, as it is specially formulated for use on vinyl and will not bleed. NEVER use actual lipstick to freshen doll's lips or cheek blush—it will very often eventually bleed into the vinyl.

RESTORING HAIR

Murphy's Oil Soap restores moisture to dried-out doll hair, as do many of the commercial conditioners on the market. For extremely dried-out and frizzy hair, as is often found on Candi and Chatty Baby, for example—Mane and Tail Conditioner, a true wonder, or a lanolin-based conditioner can be applied generously and then covered tightly with a plastic bag. Place the afflicted doll in a closet and try to forget about her for a month or two, giving the conditioner a chance to really soak in. The hair will absorb the moisture over time. Rinse thoroughly. Do not use this method on glued-on wigs

Downy Fabric Softener—the yellow formula—is great for general softening of a doll's hair. The blue formula Downy can stain the lighter hair colors.

To restore curl to saran and other synthetic doll hair (not for mohair or yarn), tightly roll each curl on a permanent wave roller or sponge roller in your choice of size, and then use an eyedropper to apply BOILING water on each curl. The heat from the boiling water will give a strong and lasting hold to each curl. Allow to dry thoroughly—at least 48 hours.

RESTORING CLOTHING

First, carefully re-sew loose snaps, buttons, lace trim, etc. Check seams, zippers, shoulder straps, and so on.

Efferdent Denture Cleaner is an excellent way to clean vintage doll clothing—it is very gentle and very thorough. About two tablets in a typical bathroom sink half full of cold water ought to do it. Use your judgment as to what fabrics to use this method on. Simple cottons are the best. Any questions or concerns—try a tiny corner first.

Think twice about submerging in water any early Mattel outfit that is red. Mattel's early red was anything but colorfast. The fur jacket of Barbie's Ice Breaker, especially, should not be washed at all, under any circumstances—the red lining will bleed on to the white fur. Barbie's 1964 Crisp and Cool should also never touch water. For clothes of this nature, try dry cleaning.

RESTORING ANY METAL PARTS

If a bit of rust or general dinginess shows up on metal areas of doll accessories, try heating up a little Vaseline Petroleum Jelly, apply to area while warm, let sit for a few hours, and wipe off. This method is especially helpful on those tin doll houses we all had, and many of the older tin toys. It can actually give a boost to the original colors!

I wish you the very best of luck in uncovering some of these rarities and the utmost success in bringing them back to their glory days.

Collector's Advisory

Throughout this book you will find a series of collector's advisories. As interest in modern doll rarities has mushroomed over the last few years, so has fraud. Dolls' hair has been dyed and re-rooted, limbs have been dyed to create black dolls, brown eyes have been inserted into blonde dolls, etc. RESTORING a doll to its original form is an ethical practice. Taking a standard doll and trying to change her into an "instant rarity" is NOT restoration—it is a type of tampering that is never ethical. Even when the tampering is clearly noted on the doll's price tag, it is an ill-advised practice, because the seller, however well intentioned, has no control over what happens to the doll once it leaves his or her hands. Odds are, that down the line, the tag will be removed and the doll will be sold by someone as a rarity for an exorbitant amount.

Please take note of these collector's advisories, as they can help you to identify a fraud and keep your doll hunts as upbeat and fun as they should be!

"Rock, child, that wonderful being that you have in your arms!"

(From the poem, *From a Child to a Doll,*
by Max Kommerell 1902-1944.
Original German title: *Inem Kind Zu Einer Puppe)*

(child pictured is Tiffin Cross—age 5)

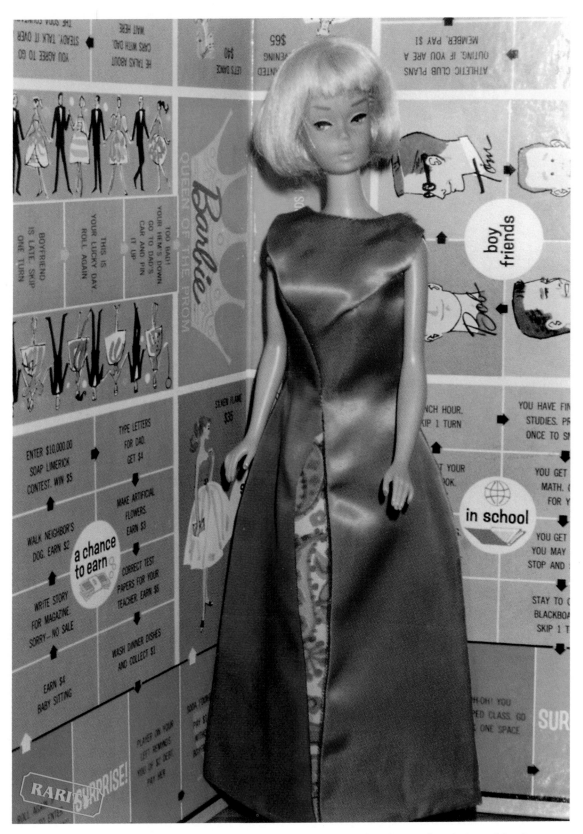

Platinum Blonde American Girl: Harder to find among American Girl Barbies is this platinum blonde variation, not to be confused with the more common lemon blonde. She is pictured here wearing "Patio Party" attire from 1965. *(Photo courtesy of Trisha Nerney.)*

BARBIE RARITIES

*A*s I begin this section on Barbie, I really wonder where to start. What can I say about this doll that hasn't already been written? Certainly, no other doll in history has had more written about her. One of these very rare combinations of the right idea at just the right time, with just the right type and amount of promotion, she has become the most popular doll of all times.

Barbie got her start as an idea that popped into the head of Ruth Handler in 1959, as she watched her daughter playing with teenage-type paper dolls, and noted that her daughter (named Barbie) always favored these teenage dolls, with their fashions and activities, over her baby and toddler dolls. Instead of cutouts, why not have one of these intriguing teenage characters in a three-dimensional format? Her husband, Elliot, owner of Mattel Toys, agreed, and by the end of that year, Barbie, in all her splendor, was featured at the Toy Fair. The rest, to coin a phrase, is history. By the time 1967 rolled around, over 500 million dollars worth of Barbies and related paraphernalia were sold. Barbie dolls were being toted from house to house, in special carrying cases bearing her name, for countless hours of a type of rapturous immersion that few who haven't experienced it can understand.

To understand the Barbie rarities that have sprung up over her years of production, it's best to start with an overview of the standard Barbies that have been manufactured since 1959:

Ponytail Barbie (1959): These early dolls are categorized by their order of production, numbers 1 to 6, with the #1's being the hardest to find and the most costly. There are variations in things such as eye paint and vinyl types that distinguish the six different ponytail Barbies. The most common hair color was blonde, second was brunette, and third was red. They all come in the now famous black and white striped strapless swimsuit, with sunglasses, earrings and pumps.

Bubble-Cut Barbie (1962): Wearing the short and bouffant "bubble" hairdo, which was so popular during this era, this doll came in black, brown, blonde and red hair colors, with varying shades of eye shadow and lipstick. The dolls originally came attired in a red knit one-piece bathing suit and red pumps.

Fashion Queen Barbie (1963): Sometimes referred to as "Bald Barbie," she had molded brown hair in a bun style, and came with three interchangeable wigs, a metallic gold and white striped strapless swimsuit, and matching turban.

A beautiful example of the
Midnight Color Magic Barbie.
(Photo courtesy of Trisha Nerney.)

Swirl Barbie (1964): This was another ponytail Barbie, but she had straight bangs that swung to the side, instead of the tight curly bangs of the first ponytail dolls. She had the same red bathing suit and pumps as the bubble-cut Barbies.

American Girl Barbie: Also called Bend-Leg Barbie, she was, as you might guess, the first Barbie with bendable legs. Her most distinguishing feature is her short pageboy hairstyle, parted in the middle.

Miss Barbie (1964): Easy to pick out in a crowd, as she had sleep eyes (eyes that open and close). Like the Fashion Queen doll, she had molded hair with interchangeable wigs.

Color Magic Barbie (1965): Both the hair and the swimsuit on this doll could change colors! With a special solution, Golden Blonde Color Magic Barbie could change to Scarlet Flame, and Midnight Black could change to Ruby Red. She came in a one-piece swimsuit decorated in a diamond pattern, and the individual diamonds could change colors. She had long, straight, side-parted hair in shades that were much less natural looking than the other Barbies.

Twist & Turn Barbie (1966): With a swivel waist and a variety of swimsuits, she was the first Barbie to have real eyelashes. Her hair was either long and straight, or in a shoulder-length flip.

The #1 Barbie: The first Barbie doll (above)
was sold in 1959, stock #850. She is also
shown here as **"Beautiful Bride."**
(Left photo courtesy of Dieter Jeschke;
right photo courtesy of Trisha Nerney.)

THE #1 BARBIE

The first Barbie doll was sold in 1959, stock #850. She has a very
light skin tone, red lips and nails, arched eyebrows, white irises with thick
black eyeliner and was marked "BARBIE TM/PATS. PEND./
cMCMLVIII/BY/MATTEL/INC." Her most distinguishing feature is the holes in
her feet which contain cooper tubing that fits around the prongs of her
circular stand. She came originally in the famous black and white striped
swimsuit, gold loop earrings, black open-toed heels and sunglasses. She is
also shown here as "Beautiful Bride."

#2 Brunette in "Gay Parisienne." *(Photo courtesy of Trisha Nerney.)*

1959 Pink silouette box, dressed display **#1 Barbie,** blonde, wearing outfit #964 "Gay Parisienne." *(Photo courtesy of Dieter Jeschke.)*

Beautiful brunette bubble cut in **"Mood for Music."** *(Photo courtesy of Trisha Nerney.)*

DRESSED DISPLAY DOLLS

In 1959 and 1960, some Barbies were packaged in pink "TM" or "R" silhouette boxes for use as store displays, and instead of the usual swimsuit, the dolls came dressed in complete outfits. Each box had a label with the name and 800 stock number of the outfit. The #3 and #4 ponytail Barbies that came as dressed display dolls are very hard to find, and the #2 ponytail Barbies that came as dressed display dolls are extremely hard to find. A #1 ponytail (distinguished by the holes in her feet) dressed in the #972 Wedding Day Set is a bona fide treasure to unearth.

LATER DRESSED DISPLAY DOLLS

In 1963 & 1964, Mattel also issued some dressed box dolls. Here is a beautiful brunette bubble cut in "Mood for Music."

THE SIDE-PART AMERICAN GIRL

The Bend Leg Barbies or "American Girls" came with pert pageboy hair styles with center parts. These 1965 and 1966 variations gave Barbie a side part and a lot of distinction in the arena of collectible Barbies. A side-part American Girl can be worth four to five times the amount of a standard 1965 or 1966 American Girl. The 1965 side-part Barbie had more subtle make up, while the 1966 doll had red cheek color and lips.

JAPANESE SIDE-PART

Made specifically for the Japanese market, with a very few sold in Europe, this doll used either the same vinyl used for Twist & Turn Barbies, which is a pinkish color, or came in a more standard tannish color vinyl; and with either straight or bendable legs. They have been found with ash brown, ash blonde, pale blonde, frosty blonde, strawberry blonde, and jet black hair. All of the Japanese side-parts came with aqua ribbon headbands.

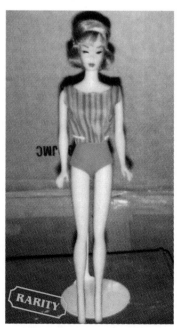

Japanese Side-Part Barbie.
(Photo courtesy of Lisa Scherzer.)

American Girl with Color Magic Face wearing one of the scarce 1600 outfits from 1965-66 called "Gold-N-Glamour." *(Photo courtesy of Trisha Nerney.)*

Side-Part Bubble-Cut Barbie.
(Photo courtesy of Trisha Nerney.)

American Girl with Color Magic Face

Most American Girls had rather subtle skin coloring and makeup. A very few were made with the more intense Color Magic face (the face normally used on the #1150 Color Magic dolls with the changing hair color). They are called "high color" among collectors and are considered hard to find. This doll is wearing one of the scarce 1600 outfits from 1965-66 called "Gold-N-Glamour."

Side-Part Bubble-Cut Barbie

Made in 1965, the simple addition of a part on the right side of Barbie's bubble cut makes her a true rarity. These side-part bubble cuts are usually found with pale yellow lipstick and light aqua eye shadow.

Platinum Blonde Swirl with White Lipstick.

(Photo courtesy of Trisha Nerney.)

BROWNETTE BUBBLE CUT

Pictured is the rarest Bubble hair color: Brownette. Lighter in tone than the standard brunette, she is much harder to find.

PLATINUM BLONDE SWIRL WITH WHITE LIPSTICK

The combination of platinum hair and white lips is a hard-to-find variation, which makes this particular Swirl Ponytail Barbie, made in 1964, stand out from the others.

The rarest Bubble hair color: Brownette. *(Photo courtesy of Trisha Nerney.)*

THE JAPANESE MIDGE

Perhaps the rarest of all Barbie Family dolls, the Japanese Midge has a totally different face and head mold than the U.S./European Midge doll. With molded hair, brown wig and eyes, and light turquoise eye shadow to match her swimsuit, she is an item most Barbie collectors have never had the opportunity to see. She is shown at right wearing outfit #1615 "Saturday Matinee." She came originally with a black pedestal stand with the name MIDGE embossed in gold.

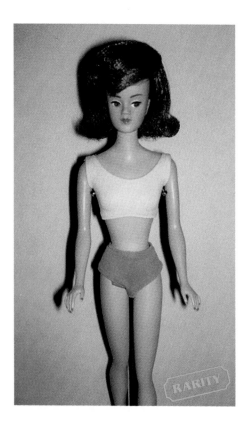

Two examples of the **Japanese Midge.** *(Photos courtesy of Dieter Jeschke.)*

Twist 'N Turn Bubble Cut.
(Photo courtesy of Dieter Jeschke.)

TWIST 'N TURN BUBBLE CUT

It's a shame that this prototype Barbie from 1966 was never mass produced, because the bubble-cut hairstyle beautifully frames the doe-like eyes and the rosebud mouth of the Twist 'N Turn face. A transition doll, she has a bit of the early '60s vintage look, and a bit of the mod era. The outfit, designed by Charlotte Johnson, is also a prototype.

BARBIE TRANSISTOR RADIO

Extremely rare 1962 child's transistor radio and patent leather storage case, covered with great early-Barbie graphics. Marked both Vanity Fair and Mattel.

Extremely rare 1962 child's transistor radio and patent leather storage case.
(Photos courtesy of Dieter Jeschke.)

INTERNATIONAL MARKET ONLY BARBIE DOLLS

Some Barbie Family dolls were never available in the U.S., even though a few of them completed sets that were sold in this country, such as Baywatch Teresa and Butterfly Ken (pictured). The several dolls which follow were sold in Mattel's International Market countries only and are provided courtesy of Melody Gocher.

The Winter Sports Barbie and Ken dolls were available at Penny's and FAO Schwartz, but the Winter Sports Midge doll (left) was only available abroad. Dance Moves Midge (right) has the Barbie name on the box, but uses the Midge head mold. Also never available in this country.

International Butterfly Ken.
(Photo courtesy of Melody Gocher.)

Please note: There have been reports of a few Winter Sports Midge dolls appearing at Toys R Us stores on the East Coast as of January 1996.

Two Style Barbie dolls (left, next page) and Baywatch Teresa (right, next page), available in International Market countries only.

Winter Sports Midge doll (left); **Dance Moves Midge** (right). *(Photos courtesy of Melody Gocher.)*

Two different **Style Barbie dolls** (left); **Baywatch Teresa** (right). *(Photos courtesy of Melody Gocher.)*

Gala Abend, which is the European version of Golden Glory. *(Photo courtesy of Trisha Nerney.)*

Midnight Blue, with its European counterpart, **Midnight Pink.** *(Photo courtesy of Trisha Nerney.)*

EUROPEAN OUTFITS

The 1966 side part (lower left) is wearing a beautiful brocade, Gala Abend, which is the European version of Golden Glory. At the lower right is Midnight Blue, with its European counterpart, Midnight Pink. Gala Abend and Midnight Pink were never sold in this country.

REDHEAD TWIST & TURN BARBIE

Made in 1967, this Twist & Turn Barbie had hard-to-find red hair. Her hair color along with her vivid face paint is an absolutely gorgeous combination. She came originally in the Twist & Turn orange swimsuit with the white net overblouse. Here, she is wearing "Beautiful Blues," a giftset outfit from Christmas 1967. As it was available for only one Christmas, this doll is extremely rare today.

#1070 CINNAMON BEND-LEG BARBIE

This doll sometimes had the Color Magic face with the American Girl pageboy hairstyle and body and was produced in 1966. What makes her rare is her unusual "cinnamon" hair color, which should be noted on her box. This distinctive tint looks just like the combination of cinnamon and sugar that gets sprinkled on toast.

Redhead Twist & Turn Barbie.
(Photo courtesy of Trisha Nerney.)

#1070 Cinnamon Bend Leg Barbie.
(Photo courtesy of Trisha Nerney.)

Hair Happenin's Barbie.
(Photo courtesy of Trisha Nerney.)

Trade-In Barbie, In the Box and
Yellow Package Barbie Play Ring.
(Photo courtesy of Lisa Scherzer.)

HAIR HAPPENIN'S BARBIE

There is some debate as to whether this doll was a 1969 Sears Christmas Exclusive, or a 1971 general issue—regardless, she is extremely rare. Shown here redressed, she has a stark and stylish short pageboy in brilliant tones of copper, and big blue eyes.

BARBIE SINGS

Another very hard to find Barbie item is this 45-rpm record set, entitled "Barbie Sings!" Six songs are included on three 45-rpm records, and the cover opens into a book which lists the songs' lyrics and includes some great early Barbie artwork! Made in 1961, the singers were Charlotte Austin and Bill Cunningham, who were accompanied by the Daniel-Darby Orchestra.

MATTEL TRADE-IN BARBIE, IN THE BOX

Twist 'N Turn Trade-In Box, next to the very rare Barbie Play Ring on the yellow card! Issued in 1967, this Barbie, whose stock number was #1162, was a trade-in promotion used as a means to introduce the American public to the new line of Twist & Turn Barbies with swivel waist, bendable legs, and real eyelashes. For $1.50 and any old doll as a trade in, you could take this beauty home. Rarity in this case refers to a doll in her original Trade-In box.

YELLOW PACKAGE BARBIE PLAY RING

In 1962 and 1963, Cleinman & Sons of Providence, Rhode Island, made thousands of adjustable play rings with the Barbie name. ("A touch of jeweled glamour for every Barbie fan.") Most of these rings were sold on a pink and blue card. Those sold on the yellow card with a picture of a redheaded ponytail Barbie are very hard to find and are worth almost twice as much. (Stock #7000).

"Barbie Sings!"
45-rpm record set.
Cover opens
into a book.
*(Photos courtesy of
LaWahna Eldred.)*

THE GENUINE MINK

Sold only by Sears during 1964 and 1965, this was a genuine "autumn haze" mink stole that had coordinated silk lining and was tagged "Barbie." The mink is being worn by a rare Cinnamon Side-Part American Girl, over outfit #1664 "Shimmering Magic" from 1966-67.

BARBIE COMIC BOOKS

Only five issues were printed in this 1962-63 series by Dell. Like the greeting cards, many of them probably found their way into the garbage can, and are therefore very hard to come by today.

The Genuine Mink.
(Photo courtesy of Dieter Jeschke.)

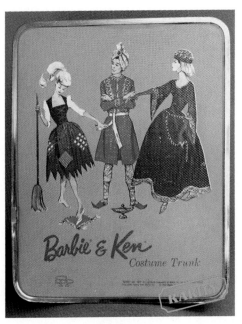

Barbie Greeting Cards. Card on left reads: "For a Sweet Niece on her Birthday." Card on right reads: "A Valentine for a Darling Daughter." *(Photo courtesy of Lisa Scherzer.)*

Barbie & Ken Costume Trunk.
(Photo courtesy of Jeanne Beaumont.)

BARBIE GREETING CARDS

Between 1963 and 1964, a variety of both birthday and Valentine's Day cards, with photos of Barbie and friends, were printed by American Greetings. As cards are often considered disposable, these are hard to come by today.

BARBIE & KEN COSTUME TRUNK

Also made by Standard Plastic Products, and very hard to find, is this Costume Trunk dated "1964 Mattel," and referred to by some collectors as the "Little Theater Trunk." The case is banded in metal, and has an interior of molded plastic, with spaces for two dolls and a third space that holds Barbie's wig stand. The cover artwork shows Barbie as Poor Cinderella, Ken as Arabian Knights, and Barbie as Guinevere.

Barbie Stationery.
(Photo courtesy of Lisa Scherzer.)

BARBIE STATIONARY

This is an extremely rare item. Made in 1964, the box front shows the profile of a Swirl Ponytail Barbie with the words "Barbie Letters!"

BARBIE & SKIPPER TRAVEL TRUNK

This is a rare Barbie case, dated 1965. Made by Standard Plastic Products, the right half of the inside compartment has room for three dolls, and the left side has a hanging rod and two accessory drawers. The Mattel name appears on the case, indicating that it was a licensed product.

THE BARBIE "SHOPS BY PHONE" SET

Probably because of all of the small components, very few of these sets have remained intact enough to make an intact appearance on today's collector market. They are extremely hard to find. Made during an era when you could ring-up the local grocery store with your order, this 1962 playset by Irwin included Barbie-sized boxes of name brand groceries, such as Domino Sugar and Kellogg's Corn Flakes, and a play phone.

KOKUSAI BOEKI BARBIE/HOUSE SET

Made for the Japanese market in 1967, this cardboard "house" held a Twist & Turn Barbie, a television and an armchair. Considered very rare.

NO FRECKLES MIDGE

No one seems to know why a 1963 Midge will show up once in a very blue moon with no freckles, as these freckles were her trademark. Nonetheless, she is a gorgeous doll with beautiful skin coloring. (Please beware! A few collectors have discovered how to remove the freckles from a standard Midge. Know the person you are buying from.)

Collector's Advisory

ACCESSORY ALERT!! *With the exception of some rarities, most Barbie cases aren't worth much. They were plentiful in their time and aren't often sought out by today's collectors. Sometimes they are even given away free by dealers as an incentive to buy other vintage Barbie items. If you do get one, DON'T toss it in the corner of a closet too quickly. With all Barbie cases, as well as Tammy cases, Kiddle cases, etc., look carefully in all nooks, crannies and crevices. Tiny accessories can settle into tiny corners and sit there for years! You may be find a Barbie closed-toe pump, Ken's alarm clock, or Kampy Kiddle's skillet! REMEMBER—the reason so many of these little personal effects are so pricey today is that they were small and easily lost years ago!*

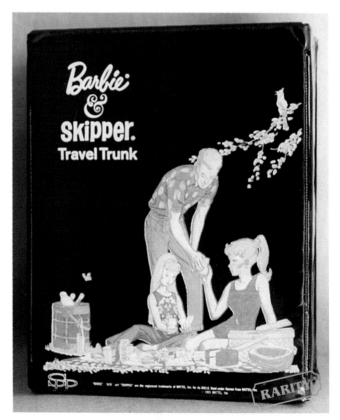

Barbie & Skipper Travel Trunk.
(Photo courtesy of Jeanne Beaumont.)

A Few Additional Notes on Barbie Rarities

1) It is believed that blonde #1 Ponytail Barbies outnumbered brunettes 3 to 1.

2) A few of the #3 Ponytail Barbies had brown eyeliner, but most had blue. Thus far, the market has not seen much of a difference in value.

3) Some Barbies in 1961 may have had a different color striped bathing suit (other than black and white). The following colors have been verbally reported: navy and white, pink and white, light blue and white, and coral and white. I find this particularly intriguing! It is my gut reaction that these color variations may be from Barbie wanna-be's like Babs or Babette. As with any of these rarities, if you own any of these alternate color bathing suits, please send a photo to me in care of the publisher! (Note: they must be tagged "Barbie"!)

4) The 1962 (painted hair) Ken usually had red swim trunks made of a strong cotton poplin material, but a few have been found made of a red cotton knit.

5) Almost all Midge dolls had straight-gazing eyes—a rare few had side-glancing.

6) "Living Barbie" was a very poseable doll who made her debut in 1970. She had a moveable waist, arms, legs, hands, neck, knees, wrists, ankles, and elbows. The great majority of these Living Barbies were made in Taiwan, but the Living Barbie that was included in the Sears exclusive "Action Accents" Gift Set is marked "Japan."

7) Barbie's Boudoir Clock was a round, child-sized wall clock with a clear plastic scalloped border.

8) Also extremely rare are the Barbie Photo Clock (white rectangular plastic frame with a blue face), and the Barbie Pendant Watch.

9) Casey Hair Variations are another source of bewilderment to collectors! Casey was introduced in 1967, was Francie's size and had outstandingly attractive facial features. The uniform hairstyle for these early Caseys (not the "baggies" of 1975) was a very short, straight pageboy—either flat or fluffy (for store display dolls). An occasional oddity will pop up with very curly hair. These types of one-in-a-million variations are not unusual for Mattel!

10) Also hard to find is the Midge Wig Wardrobe (#1009). The set, introduced in 1965, included a Midge head with short molded hair and orange headband, a wig stand, and three wigs—blonde, brunette and red.

CURRENT HARD-TO-FIND BARBIES

"Math Is Tough"
Teen Talk Barbie (1993)

A total of 270 phrases were created for the campily-clad Teen Talk Barbie issued in 1993. Each Teen Talk doll that was manufactured spoke only four phrases, randomly selected from the original 270 possibilities. About one percent of these dolls utters the terribly politically incorrect phrase—"Math class is tough!"—supposedly perpetuating the myth that chicks are bad in math. This forbidden phrase was subsequently deleted from the list, and not put into Teen Talk Barbies that were to come, but the dolls already in the stores remainded on the shelves. Current value for these "Math is Tough Teen Talks" has skyrocketed. This is one of the few current Barbies that need not remain in the box to retain its value, as she has to be taken out to install the batteries that enable her to talk.

Other hard-to-find
Barbie dolls include:

✦ All Braniff Airlines and Singapore Airlines Special Issue Barbies.

✦ Blossom Beautiful; Sears Exclusive, 1992; not a limited edition, but hard to find.

✦ Porcelain Blonde Gay Parisiennet; Disney 1991; limited to 300.

✦ Porcelain Redhead Gay Parisienne; Disney 1991; limited to 300.

✦ Porcelain Blonde Plantation Belle; Disney 1992; limited to 300.

✦ Porcelain Brunette Crystal Rhapsody; Disney 1992; limited to 250.

✦ Porcelain Blonde Silken Flame; Disney 1993; limited to 400.

No Bangs Francie. *(Doll courtesy of Eugenia Kurz. Photo by the author.)*

FRANCIE RARITIES

Among the army of boyfriends, girlfriends and mere acquaintances of Barbie's, Francie proudly takes her place among the ranks as Barbie's cousin. Introduced in 1966, Francie ushered in the "Eyelash Era," as collectors call it, and offered children more of a "frying size" Barbie to play with. Slightly smaller in stature, and with fewer curves, she may have been Mattel's response to the success of Ideal's youthful ingenue—Tammy.

In her first year, both bend-leg (#1130) and straight-leg (#1140) Francie versions were manufactured. Later years brought later Francies: the Twist & Turn (#1170) in 1967; Francie with Growin' Pretty Hair (#1129) and Francie Hair Happenin's (#1122), both in 1970; Malibu Francie (#1068) in 1971, which was made from the Casey head mold; New Francie with Growin' Pretty Hair (#1074), also in 1971; Busy Francie (#3312) in 1972; Quick Curl Francie (#4222) in 1973; and "Baggie" Francie (sold economically in a plastic bag, #7699) in 1975.

Very popular in her day, the Francie doll was produced in sufficient quantities that legions of them are still available at doll shows and Barbie conventions, and at fairly reasonable prices.

A few Francies, however, rise above the commonplace like sweet cream at the top of a milk bottle, because of their short production runs. These are the Francies that die-hard Barbie collectors angle for, bob for, dig and delve for. Perhaps the thrill is in the hunt; or perhaps, as in the case of the 1971 No Bangs Francie, some of these dolls stand out for their unique beauty. Whatever the case, the price tags on these rare Francies reflect a lot of enthusiasm on the part of collectors.

NO BANGS FRANCIE

Made in 1971, as both a blonde and brunette, this highly valued find is made of Twist & Turn vinyl, giving her complexion a beautiful and soft, luminous quality. Her hair is brushed straight back from her forehead, with no part, and falls in a shoulder-length flip. The omission of bangs shows off the narrow, graceful lines of her face.

1967 Black Francie (left);
1968 Black Francie (right).
(Dolls courtesy of Euginia Kurz. Photos by the author.)

1967 BLACK FRANCIE

Considered hard to find are both the 1967 and 1968 Black Francies. Typical of the day, they are simply darkened versions of the white dolls, with no outstanding ethnic features. The 1967 Black Francies have hair that has, over the years, oxidized to a reddish color. The dolls also have beautiful bright terra cotta colored eyes, and bright coral lips.

1968 BLACK FRANCIE

The 1968 Black Francies have retained their original hair color—a deep black—and their eyes are more of a chocolate brown. The doll is pictured here in her original box and dressed in the multi-print suit that was usually on the 1967 Black Francies.

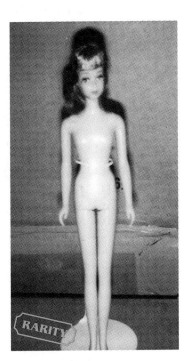

Japanese Francie.
(Photo courtesy of Lisa Scherzer.)

JAPANESE FRANCIE

Sold on the Japanese market in 1967, Japanese Francie sports the same eyelashes and hairstyle as the American Francies produced at that time, but has one outstanding component—blue eyes. All other commonplace Francies, except the Malibu's, had brown eyes.

SKIPPER RARITIES

*T*here have been a lot of famous sister acts in our culture. The Andrew Sisters, the Lennon Sisters, Dear Abby and Ann Landers, among them. However, it is unlikely that anyone has ever spent more time in her sister's shadow than Skipper has spent in Barbie's!

She arrived on the scene in 1964, at 9½ inches, and was available as either a blonde, brunette or redhead. These very first Skippers have a separate look from all the other Skippers that followed them over the years, and are easy for a trained eye to pick out in a crowd. They are, of course, all vinyl, with straight, non-bendable legs; and have long straight hair with bangs, held back with a headband.

In the first year, ten outfits were issued for Skipper; 1965 brought fourteen more, not including four accessory packs and one gift set, "Skipper on Wheels" (#1032). In 1966, twelve more Skipper outfits were produced.

The 1964 Skipper is considered by most collectors to be the most attractive of the models and is therefore the most sought after. Her marketplace values, however, are mere fractions of Barbie's. Some of the Skippers that followed the 1964 version are:

Bendable Leg Skipper (1965): Just like the 1964 Skipper, but with bendable legs. Came in red, white and blue nautical-look swimsuit. Most came in an enclosed box. Those that came in open-faced boxes are considered rare.

1964 Skipper.

The first **Skipper** and
Skooter dolls.
(Photo by the author.)

Twist & Turn Skipper (1968): Jointed at the waist, she had the same hair-style as the first two Skippers, but came with a blue elastic headband instead of brass. She wore a pink and blue skirted swimsuit.

Pose & Play Skipper (1972): With "swinging free" arms that allowed her some gymnastic maneuvers, she had short curly pigtails tied with blue ribbons, real eyelashes, and a blue and white checked playsuit.

Quick Curl Skipper (1973): The first Skipper with freckles, she had a long pageboy-style hairdo, which was easily curled, and wore a long blue and white checked cotton dress, similar to the other Barbie Quick Curl fami-ly members. Deluxe Quick Curl Skipper had a long pink granny-gown-style dress with a crochet-look shawl. Both are beautiful dolls.

Growing Up Skipper (1975): This Skipper not only gained $3/4$ of an inch in height, but could develop an instant bustline, by a turn of her left arm. She wore a red body suit, two red and white checkered wrap-around

Super Teen Skipper.
(Photo by the author.)

skirts—one long and one short—and platform shoes. The first issue had a long, blonde, fuller hairdo and the second issue had shorter hair. Despite protests from some women's lib groups, the doll was a big seller.

Super Teen Skipper (1979): Another attempt at making Skipper older, she was a short-lived experiment. Her arms were bent at the elbow like the modern Barbie doll, and she originally came packaged with skateboard gear and a change of evening clothes.

Soon Skipper was back to being a preteen. This seems to be the look most consumers are comfortable with, as it continues through to the most current Skippers. Today's Skippers are dressed in a more mature and sophisticated manner, just as today's youth is, but they remain preteens, nonetheless. Almost all Skippers from 1980 on can be picked up at very reasonable cost in the secondary market.

SKIPPER RARITIES

The Japanese Skipper

Made specifically for the Japanese market during the 1960s, this doll has the same look and markings of the 1964 Skipper, but has brown eyes with triangular-shaped highlights on the sides, similar to the eyes we see on Speed Racer and other Japanese cartoon characters.

Blonde "Baggie"
Pose & Play Skipper

Sold in plastic bags, rather than boxes, during 1975, the blonde version of these "baggie" dolls is considered rare.

1970 Re-issue
of 1964 Skipper

The 1970 re-issue came in the original red and white sunsuit, and had the same look and hairstyle as the first 1964 Skipper. What distinguishes this doll is a pinker skin tone than the original Skipper, and a different box which depicts 1969 and 1970 Skipper fashions.

1970 Trade-In Skipper

Used as a promotional gimmick to introduce the new line of "living" Skippers, she was $1.99, with any other doll acceptable as a trade in.

(Photo courtesy of
Lisa Scherzer.)

Barbie & Skipper
Vanity Case

A huge array of carrying cases for Barbie and Barbie family members have been made over the years. This unusual lavender-colored trunk was available only through Sears in 1964. The trunk contained two mirrored vanities and two stools. What a novel idea!

Other Skipper Rarities

◆ Barbie's Wedding Party Gift Set (#1017); issued in 1964; the set included Barbie, Ken, Midge and Skipper in wedding finery and is currently valued at between $1,500 and $2,500.

◆ Skipper on Wheels Gift Set (#1032); 1965; valued currently at $700, NRFB.

◆ Dog Show (#1929), Let's Play House (#1932), and Country Picnic (#1933) outfits; mint and complete $150. Junior Bridesmaid (#1934); mint and complete $200. All issued in 1966.

◆ Skipper Bunk Beds (#4011); 1965-1967; mint/no box $125.

◆ Skipper Swing-A-Rounder Gym (#1179); 1972; mint/no box $100.

CHATTY CATHY RARITIES

We all have specific memories of the dolls that we had in childhood. We see their little faces gazing at us from a bin at a garage sale, and our past whispers to us. Chatty Cathy is unique in that, whether we owned her or not, we all seem to remember her. That's because she was promoted in a big way and had the "star quality" necessary to make it big.

If the doll-playing years of your childhood happened to fall in the early 1960s, chances are that while watching Saturday morning cartoons, you were captivated and startled by the image of two freckled-faced dolls winking at you from the TV set. Chatty Cathy (Mattel 1960) was not the first talking doll, but she was the first to be promoted with a mass blitz of TV commercials aimed directly at children. In case the memories are fuzzy, the original jingle sang out:

OH, CHATTY CATHY, OH CHATTY CATHY!
OH, MATTEL'S FAMOUS TALKING DOLL!
WE PULL THE RING AND YOU SAY ELEVEN DIFFERENT THINGS!
YOU CAN TELL IT'S MATTEL—IT'S SWELL!!

Like Hula Hoops and Barbie dolls and any other contagious form of glee that sweeps through childhood, kids all over the country were asking Mom and Dad for Chatty Cathy, staring at her image in Christmas catalogues, and singing along with the television commercials. In an epidemic of adoration, they helped to make her a master stroke of success for the Mattel Toy Company. Today, "Chatty Cathy" is a household word and generic term for any talking doll or talkative person.

How to describe her? Well, she was a twenty-inch tall, mannequin-style pull-string talker, made of hard plastic and vinyl, and came in a variety of hair colors. But what really makes her stand out in a crowd is that she was probably the first modern doll that wasn't designed to look like an idealized conception of the perfect baby or toddler. She had two protruding front teeth (her ardent fans never use the word "buck"), a tummy that showed her love of ice cream, feet that looked like the rest of her had to grow into them, and a crop of freckles dancing across her nose. She looked, in short, like a real kid. And in the early '60s, when TV moms were feather dusting in pearls and heels, realism of this sort was a relatively new concept.

The original Chatty Cathy was produced by Mattel from 1960 through 1965, and a breakdown of the three main types follows:

1960-1961: The #1 Chatty Cathy was produced only as a blonde with a soft face and cloth-covered speaker. She had hard plastic limbs, rather than the rigid vinyl limbs of the later models. The coloring on the #1 faces has a tendency to fade rather badly, and they are often found with their freckles a silvery-greenish color. Originally, she had gorgeous cheek blush, carnation pink lips and decal eyes in a few variations of blue.

Many of these first dolls are unmarked. Those that are marked read: "CHATTY CATHY TM/PATENT PENDING/MCMLX BY MATTEL INC. HAWTHORNE CALIF."

1962: At the start of 1962, cloth-covered speakers were still being used, but were later changed to a series of holes forming a hexagon in her stomach. The #2's still had soft faces, but were given the new rigid vinyl limbs. This was the year that the first brunette models were introduced, many with brown eyes. They exhibited the same short pageboy style as their blonde counterparts.

1963: The most distinctive difference in the #3 Chatty Cathys is the introduction of what collectors refer to as the "hard face," a new rigid vinyl face that replaced the soft vinyl face of the earlier models. (Note: with a soft face, you are able to squeeze the doll's cheeks inward. The hard face models have cheeks that are completely rigid.) This new hard face was considerably smaller and thinner than the earlier faces and gave Chatty a noticeably different appearance.

A group of **Black Chattys.** *(From the Ruth Kibbons collection.)*

Many collectors reject the #3's, preferring instead the classic apple-cheeked dolls of the earlier years; but some collectors actually favor the rigid vinyl faces because they have tended to hold their color better over the years. The overall skin tone, cheek color and freckles on these dolls are usually still in great condition, even when found today.

Red-haired Chatty Cathys were also introduced in 1963, as was a brand new hairstyle: pigtails.

Collector's Advisory

In attempting to date a particular Chatty Cathy doll, make note of the different head types, speaker styles, and other criteria mentioned above, but also be aware of the following. When sold new, the dolls came with a warranty offering to fix the voice mechanism within 90 days from the date of purchase for a fee of $1. Mattel repaired the defective unit by simply replacing the entire torso that contained the voice box. It is therefore not impossible to find a head style from one year attached to a torso from another year.

BROWN-EYED BLONDE

Considered the ultimate find for many serious collectors, this doll is so rare that it is difficult to gather enough data to come up with an estimated value. These dolls are assumed to be last-minute factory substitutions when the assembly line that was constructing the blonde Chatty Cathys ran out of blue eyes. They could also be the product of some incredibly bored factory worker trying to break up the monotony. Whatever their origins, they are true and unique beauties.

But first it must be determined whether the brown eyes are original. It is possible for an unscrupulous dealer or collector to insert brown eyes from a brunette Chatty in an attempt to fabricate an instant "rare" doll. One way to verify its authenticity, is to very carefully remove the doll's head to inspect the rounded, soft vinyl pockets in which the sleep eyes rest. Very often, if the eyes have been replaced, these pockets will be cut.

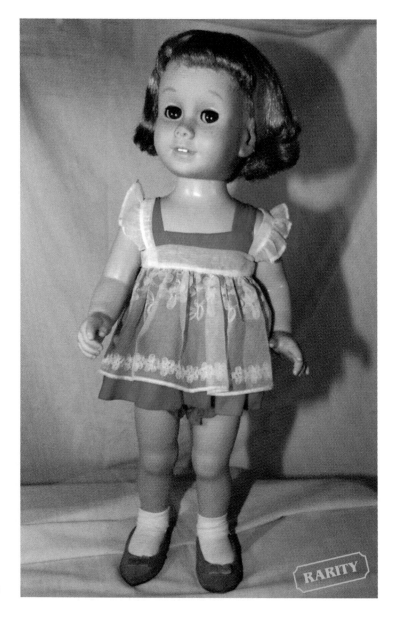

Brown-eyed Blonde.
(Doll courtesy of Tara Wood.
Photo by Paul Carranza.)

RARITY

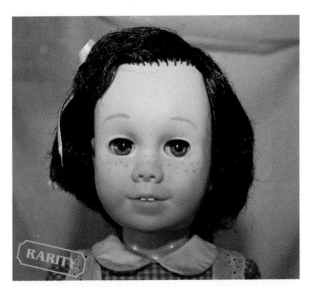

Olive-Eyed Chatty Cathy.
(Doll courtesy Tara Wood.
Photo by Paula Carranza.)

OLIVE-EYED CHATTY CATHY

The term "rare" only scratches the surface when it comes to describing this doll. This is a Chatty Cathy with true black hair and beautiful olive-colored eyes. No collector contacted in the course of researching this book had even heard of the existence of any type of green-eyed Chatty Cathy. According to the owner, the eyes show no signs of ever having been replaced, and from their uniform coloring, it is obvious that they are not brown eyes that have turned green due to the type of oil damage that can occur during restoration. A rare and reigning beauty, she is wearing the harder-to-find blue gingham party dress.

BLACK CHATTY CATHY

Mattel also produced an African American Chatty Cathy. The doll had comparatively limited distribution and now enjoys much higher prices on the collector's market. A Black Chatty Cathy with a pageboy haircut is a rare and coveted find among collectors, but a Black Chatty Cathy with pigtails is the proverbial pot at the end of the rainbow. The Black Chatty Cathys do not have African American features, but are simply dyed versions of the white dolls, with soft, straight, black hair, and brown eyes and eyelids.

**Black Chatty
Cathy Dolls.**
*(Photo courtesy of
Ruth Kibbons.)*

More examples of **Black Chattys.**
(Dolls courtesy of Tara Wood. Photo by Paula Carranza.)

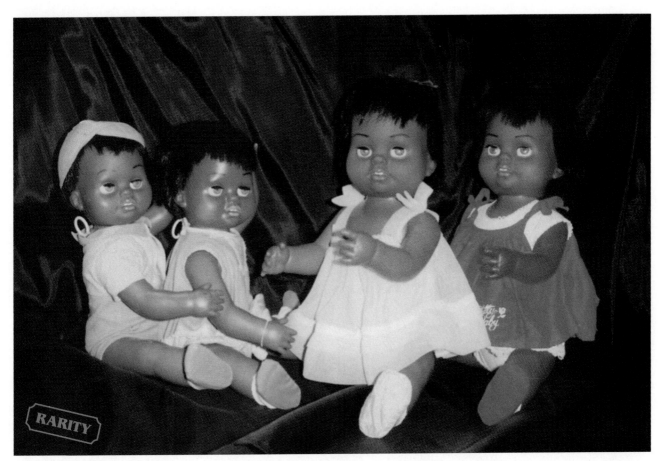

RARITY

Black Chatty Babies.
(Photo courtesy of Ruth Kibbons.)

Black Chatty Babies

For a long time, it has been believed that a Black Tiny Chatty Brother was never made. Don't let this picture fool you—we still haven't found one! The doll to the far left is actually a Tiny Chatty Baby (girl), wearing a Tiny Chatty Brother romper from a white doll. "He" is seated here with a Black Tiny Chatty Baby (both are fifteen-inches tall, and she is wearing original clothes), and two beautiful examples of Black Chatty Babies (both are eighteen-inches tall and in original outfits). The wonderful condition of these dolls makes them even more rare.

Chatty with Charmin' Hair

Here is a true abnormality. This is a Chatty Cathy doll with Charmin' Chatty Hair. The texture and tones (a mixture of standard blonde, platinum and brown) identify it as Charmin' hair, and how it wound up on Cathy's head is anybody's guess. Her body markings ("U.S. Pat 3,017, 187/Other U.S. and Foreign Pats. Pend/Pat'd in Canada 1962") show that she is from the latter years of production, which is the time period encompassing most of these curious variations.

Note: she is wearing Sunday Visit, a harder-to-find original outfit.

Two views of
**Chatty with
Charmin' Hair.**
*(Doll courtesy of
Tara Wood. Photos
by Paula Carranza.)*

HAIR COLOR VARIATIONS

Although it is difficult to tell from the photography, both of these dolls have highly unusual hair shades for Chatty Cathys. The hard-faced pigtail on the left has a chestnut brown shade (I currently know of only one in the hands of a collector), and the soft-faced page-boy on the right has streaked or "frosted" hair, with shades of brown and blonde mixed in. Hair texture is Cathy's—not Charmin's. Two collectors known to the author have each reported owning one of these frosted-hair Chattys.

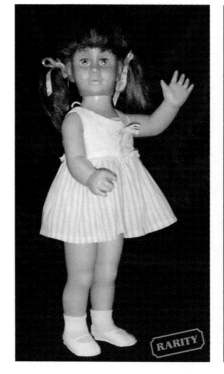
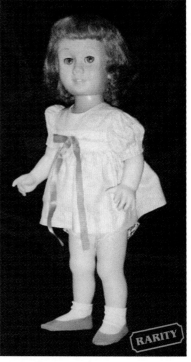

(Photos courtesy of Ruth Kibbons.)

Frosted-hair Chatty Cathy.
(Doll courtesy of Tara Wood.
Photo by Paula Carranza.)

HAIR COLOR VARIATIONS

Here is another example of a frosted-hair Chatty Cathy; this one with white streaks that are mixed in with the standard blonde. Her carnation pink lips, and freckles and eyebrows that have faded to a gray-green color, all seem to indicate that her head was among the very earliest to be manufactured. Mattel advertised Chatty Cathy as looking like a real child, having, among other things, a mixture of more than one hair color, just as real children do. Perhaps this doll, with her starkly contrasting hair colors, was part of an experimental stage before Mattel arrived at the ideal hairshade combinations that were to be used to achieve the realism they were after.

Strawberry Blonde
Chatty Cathy.
(Photo by the author.)

STRAWBERRY BLONDE

These little beauties are "sleepers" right now, as most collectors and dealers have not yet taken note of their existence. These dolls are not standard redheads, nor standard blondes, but instead have blonde hair with a district reddish cast. Holding one next to a standard blonde example will help to confirm this. Although extremely rare, strawberry blonde Chatty Cathys are priced the same as standard Chattys because relatively few collectors and dealers are aware of them. If you come cross one, grab it! These dolls appear to have a bright future!

A strawberry blonde **Chatty Cathy** (left) next to a standard blonde version.
(Photo by the author.)

Collector's Advisory

Strawberry Blonde Chatty Cathy dolls were very rare up until the time that I first wrote about them in the spring of 1995. Soon after, they started showing up in greater numbers. This is rather curious, to say the least, so PLEASE—check the doll's scalp carefully to see if there is any discoloration, as there is a good chance that some of these newly unearthed Strawberry Blondes have had their hair either dyed or rinsed. The vinyl on the scalp is porous enough to absorb some of the dye and can help you spot a fraud!

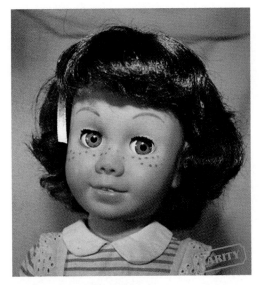

(Doll courtesy of Tara Wood. Photo by Paula Carranza.)

Here is an absolutely mint and gorgeous example of some of the delightful novelties that came out of the latter years of Chatty Cathy's production. This doll is a brunette (in the auburn family), with a striking set of bright federal blue eyes, with purple flecks that rim the outside edges. The author, and one other collector known to her, own Tiny Chatty Babies—one blonde and one brunette—that have these purple flecks in their eyes. In addition to her distinctive hair and eye colors, this doll is a soft-faced auburn—another rarity. Thanks to Tara Wood for displaying this most unique doll!

ROOTING VARATION

Another delightful curiosity is this later-issue Chatty Cathy with the bright federal blue-purple fleck eye color combination and true black hair drawn up into pigtails. Her hair is rooted only at the hairline, and down the center part that forms the pigtails. All other examples of pig-tailed Chatty Cathys have hair that is rooted all over the head.

(Doll courtesy of Tara Wood. Photo by Paula Carranza.)

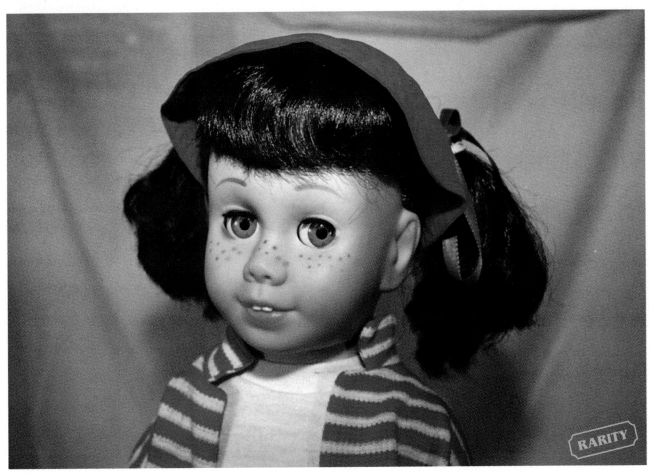

AMBER-EYED CHATTY CATHY

Amber eyes are another hard-to-find eye color variation among Chattys. This Chatty Cathy is an amber-eyed brunette with true black hair, and a soft face that seems to be distinctly different from the soft face mold that we are accustomed to seeing. Could the factory have used soft vinyl in the hard vinyl face mold?

Note: This very doll sold in February of 1997 for $495.

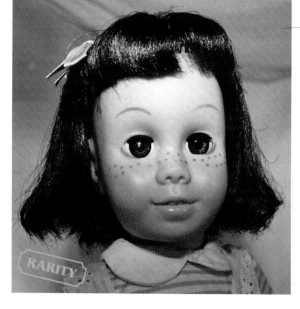

Amber-Eyed Chatty Cathy.
(Doll courtesy of Tara Wood.
Photo by Paula Carranza.)

CHATTY'S BLUE AND WHITE JUMPER

There were twelve original outfits made for Chatty Cathy, including: the pink Peppermint Stick dress; red Peppermint Stick dress; Nursery School A-line dress; red velvet Party Coat; red, white and blue Playtime outfit; red cotton Sunsuit; Sleepytime pajamas; red velvet and white lace dress made for #3 Chattys; rust and green Sunny Day capri set; pink nylon and taffeta Sunday Visit dress; blue and white checkered Party Dress; and the blue jumper.

The blue jumper was either a solid-colored dark blue or a two-toned dark top/light bottomed combination and came originally on the earliest dolls with a white cotton overblouse and tulle petticoat. One superlatively-rare variation of this dress has a dark blue top and a snow white bottom. It came with a white eyelet overblouse and white velvet shoes, and is a beautiful combination. In 1992, in a group of about 200 Chatty Cathy collectors, only two owned this dress. All Chatty Cathy clothing was originally tagged "CHATTY CATHY," but some of the tags may have fallen off over the years.

L-R: The **Two-Toned Jumper,** the **Blue and White Jumper,** and the **Solid Jumper;** all topped by the white eyelet overblouse.
(Photo by the author.)

CHATTY CATHY PENCIL POST BED

This hard-to-find piece is known as the Chatty Cathy Pencil Post Bed, which refers to the thin, tapered nature of the four posts. Made of a heavy white plastic which can show some yellowing with age, it has a round emblem on the foot board with the name "Chatty Cathy," which makes it easy to identify.

CHATTY CATHY TV TRAY

Remember eating your after-school snack in front of Huckleberry Hound, or your Rice Krispies in front of Beany and Cecil? With television sets being more plentiful today, many have found their way into the kitchen, eliminating the need for an old Baby Boom favorite—the TV tray. This particular example, licensed by Mattel and clearly marked "Chatty Cathy," is a great find for the collector. Two similar trays connected to some steel tubing and casters also resulted in a device known as the Chatty Cathy Tea Cart.

Chatty Cathy TV Tray.
(Photo courtesy of Ruth Kibbons.)

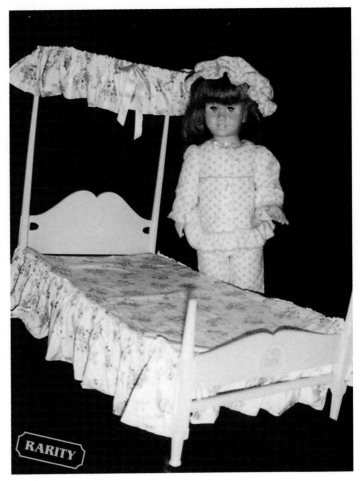

Chatty Cathy Pencil Post Bed.
(Photo courtesy of Ruth Kibbons.)

Soft-faced Chatty Cathys.

SOFT-FACED PIGTAIL

Since the pigtail hair style was not introduced until 1963, the same year that all Chatty Cathys switched to hard faces, it is not known why a pigtailed Chatty Cathy with a soft face will occasionally turn up. But they do exist, and are very much in demand by in-the-know collectors. Again, these could be products of factory substitutions. Possibly some soft faces were left over from last year's stock, and a budget-conscious production supervisor may have wanted to make sure there was no waste. These dolls are not as difficult to unearth as the brown-eyed blondes or the strawberry blondes, and they present a fun challenge for all collectors as they are almost always priced the same as any regular Chatty Cathy.

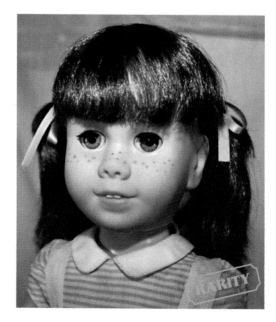

Another example of a **soft-faced pigtail.** To add to this doll's rarity, she is also an auburn. Both pigtails and auburns are extremely hard to find in the soft-face version.

More unusual Chattys. A **hard-faced pigtail** (left) with a factory curl and another beautiful example of a **soft-faced pigtail** (right). *(Dolls courtesy of Terry Carter. Photo courtesy of Patti Cooke.)*

HARD-FACED PAGEBOY

The hard-faced Chatty Cathy dolls, which were sold in the very last years, came with the pigtail hairdo. So, a hard-faced Chatty Cathy, with a pageboy hairstyle like the blonde pictured here, is an abnormality that rarely turns up. So far, there is no difference in price from a standard Chatty.

CHATTY BABY NURSERY SET

This set of cardboard bedroom furniture for the nineteen-inch Chatty Baby is very hard to come by today. Originally selling for $6.00, this stock #318 included a standing wardrobe, crib, chair and hangers, done in shades of pink.

Blonde doll on right is a hard-faced pageboy. *(Photo by the author.)*

**Chatty Baby
Nursery Set.**
*(Photo courtesy
of Ruth Kibbons.)*

THE CHATTY
PLAY TABLE

Doll accessories closely imitated the baby equipment of the day. These play tables were popular in the '60s—a place for baby to eat, read storybooks or bang their rattles incessantly. The seat on this unit made for the Chatty dolls could lift out to become a car seat or rocker. I don't know how many readers can recall this, but it was a definite thrill to bring your favorite doll along for a car trip to the grocery store or to Grandma's!

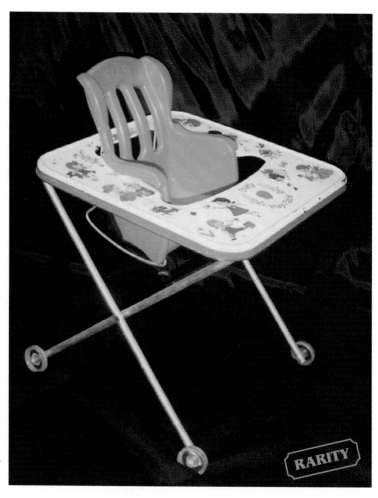

The Chatty Play Table.
*(Photo courtesy of
Ruth Kibbons.)*

Sizzly Friddle and Bunson Burnie.
(Photo by the author.)

LIDDLE KIDDLES

Impish and whimsical, precious and diminutive: nothing personifies these terms like the line of little characters Mattel started manufacturing in 1966. These incredibly popular little dolls are fondly known to tail-end Baby Boomers and Generation X-ers as Liddle Kiddles. Both their design and their accompanying accessories were detailed and imaginative. The dolls ranged in size from ³/₄-inch to 4-inches tall, and can be identified, when not found clothed, by their individual face painting. The larger Kiddles have a wire skeleton imbedded in their soft vinyl bodies making them poseable. They are marked "© Mattel Inc." The smaller Kiddles have accessories marked "Mattel," but are usually unmarked themselves.

The first series of Kiddles, issued in 1966, contained a total of nine dolls:

Babe Biddle: Dark-haired girl with her own sports car.

Liddle Diddle: Blonde baby girl with a Pebbles-style ponytail on top of her head. She came in pink checked PJs and had her own pink crib with play beads and a toy duck.

Howard "Biff" Boddle: Blonde boy with a cap and a red or yellow wagon.

Florence Niddle: Dressed as a nurse, she came with a baby and a yellow and white baby carriage.

Greta Griddle: With her own kitchen set consisting of either a yellow table and pink chairs, or a pink table and yellow chairs. Also included was a tea set, usually the same color as the chairs. She was blonde with a blue dress, with white dots.

Millie Middle: A brown-haired girl in a pink and blue sunsuit and hat. She came with a canopied sandbox, tiny pail and a shovel.

Lola Liddle: With long blonde hair blowing in the wind, she came in a nautical outfit and had her own sailboat and sailor's cap.

Howard "Biff" Boddle.
(Photo by the author.)

(L-R) **Millie Middle, Slipsy Sliddle,** and **Lola Liddle** each came with their own play accessories. *(Photo by the author.)*

Freezy Sliddle.
(Photo by the author.)

Windy Fliddle.
(Photo by the author.)

Calamity Jiddle: This little cowgirl came in two variations of hair; either yellow or platinum blonde. She wore a red jumpsuit, a white fringed vinyl skirt and an oversized black felt cowboy hat.

Bunson Burnie: A favorite with collectors, he was the Liddle Kiddle Fire Chief and had an adorable round face. He came in a yellow slicker and red fire chief's hat and had a fire engine with a ladder.

This first series of Kiddles was the only one that all came with combs and brushes. In the second series, three—Trikey Triddle, Soapy Siddle and Baby Liddle—came with hair grooming accessories.

This group was later joined by fifteen more:

Lemmons Stiddle: Came with a lemonade stand, glasses and a pitcher of lemonade.

Telly Viddle: Came with a television set with rotating pictures and a Barbie-variety box of pretzels.

Kampy Kiddle: A collector's favorite in jeans and yellow T-shirt, who came with a fishing pole, fry pan and sleeping bag.

Roly Twiddle: Black Kiddle who came with a wagon, pail and shovel.

Slipsy Sliddle: Redheaded cutie with her own pink slide.

Beddy Bye Biddle: Came with her own bed, pillow and blanket.

Pretty Piddle: Came with a vanity table and stool.

Beat-A-Diddle: A very rare and sought-after little girl with foot-length blonde hair. She wore either black flowered or hard-to-find red flowered bell bottoms, and had a microphone and guitar.

Sizzly Friddle: Wearing a blue and green dress with an attached white apron that read "yum yum," she came with a red barbecue grill with tiny connected food.

Freezy Sliddle: Gliding on her blue and white sled, she wore a blue jacket with pink fur trim, pink tights and white snow boots.

Windy Fliddle: Wearing a blue vinyl jumpsuit, yellow vinyl cap and goggles, she had her own red and yellow plane.

Trikey Triddle: In either a pink floral dress or a red and white dotted dress, she had a pink, white and blue tricycle and either a pink or yellow balloon.

Surfy Skiddle: The Kiddles' answer to Gidget, she came with a blue wave with detachable red and yellow surfboard, and a pink floral towel.

Soapy Siddle: Wearing a red and white striped robe and slippers, she had an auburn ponytail, and came with a gold plastic bathtub with cotton bubbles, talc, and a yellow towel.

Baby Liddle: A real rarity who commands top dollar in the collector's market, she is often confused with Liddle Diddle from the first series. Baby Liddle has no hair except for a top knot of blonde curls. She came in a pink dress with a matching pillow, and a blue and white buggy.

Soapy Siddle.
(Photo by the author.)

Telly Viddle.
(Photo by the author.)

Skeddle Kiddles and their Traveldiddles. Top Row (L to R): **Lickety Spliddle,** a **trikediddle, Shirley Skediddle.** Bottom Row: (L to R): A **Helididdle, Annabelle Autodiddle,** (redressed in "Posies in Pink"), a Skediddle mechanism that fits into the backs of Skediddle dolls, **Annabelle Autodiddle** (redressed in "orange Meringue") and an **Autodiddle.**

Skediddle Kiddles soon followed and are very popular with today's collectors. Skediddles could walk or peddle a riding toy when a Skediddle mechanism was inserted in their backs! Some popular Skediddles were:

Shirley Skediddle: Platinum blonde in shocking pink velvet.

Sheila Skediddle: Brunette in a yellow pleated dress.

Annabelle Autodiddle: Redhead with a lime green, orange and hot pink race car.

Harriet Helididdle: Brunette with an orange and yellow helicopter.

Tracy Trikediddle: A carrot top in an orange and yellow vinyl dress and a pink and aqua trike.

A special Skediddle gift set: Included Lickety Spliddle, a girl with a blonde pageboy who came with three "Traveldiddles"—the race car, helicopter and trike.

Later Skediddles were Swingy, Cherry Blossom, Rah Rah, Heather Hiddlehorse, Tessie Tractor and Fritzi Frostiwagon.

Jewelry Kiddles: These tiny Kiddles came in pins, rings, necklaces, and bracelets. Each was encased in a clear plastic compartment that was incorporated into jewelry that the child could wear. The dolls were an average of $3/4$-inch to 1-inch tall.

Animiddle Kiddles: These were furry Kiddle pets children could pin onto their clothes. A lion, tiger, deer and mouse were produced.

Kozmic Kiddles: These were glow-in-the-dark space aliens in their own dome-topped spaceships. These Kiddles bring top dollar on today's collector's market.

Lucky Locket Kiddles: Included Lois, Lorelei, Lottie, Louise, Luanna, Loretta, Laverne, Lou, Liz, Larkey, Lola, Lilac and Lorna. They were smaller in size, but larger than the jewelry Kiddles. They were sold in plastic lockets encrusted with tiny "jewels."

Florence Niddle hurries in.   Now there are . . .

Florence Niddle
against **Kiddle
Storybook.**
*(Photo by the
author.)*

Kola Kiddles: Each came in their own Kola bottles with cap and included Kleo Kola, Greta Grape, Laffy Lemon, Shirley Strawberry, Olivia Orange, and Luscious Lime.

Storybook Kiddles: These very hot collectibles came with detailed costumes and are taller and thinner than most other Kiddles. Each doll in this series came with its own storybook and accessories. The series included Liddle Biddle Peep with a lamb and staff; Peter Paniddle with crocodile and Tinker Bell; Alice in Wonderliddle with a white rabbit and big watch; Liddle Red Riding Hiddle with a furry wolf and basket; Liddle Middle Muffet with her tuffet, curds, whey and spider; Sleeping Biddle with a crown and royal sleeping couch; and Cinderiddle who came with both her ball gown and tatter clothing, glass slipper and broom.

Sweet Treat Kiddles: They came in either lollipop or ice cream cone plastic containers color coordinated to the Kiddles outfits. The dolls themselves were also smaller in size like the Lucky Locket Kiddles.

Kologne Kiddles: Each was scented and came in their own plastic Kologne bottles and were small in stature like the Locket Kiddles. The group included Rosebud, Violet, Honeysuckle, Sweet Pea, Lilly of the Valley, Apple Blossom, Orange Blossom, Bluebell and Gardenia. These Kiddles seem quite plentiful on the collector's market.

Tea Party Kiddles: They are probably the most ornate and elegant in the Kiddle array. This set of four came in courtly ball gowns and "up-do" hairstyles. Each were four inches tall and were sold in display domes with matching child-size tea cups and saucers. They were Lady Lace, Lady Crimson, Lady Silver and Lady Lavender.

Other novelty Kiddles included Zoolery Kiddles, who came in their own traveling animal cages; Santa Kiddle; Funny Bunny; and Luvvy Duvvy, for Valentine's Day.

Sleeping Biddle.
(Photo by the author.)

Beddy Bye Biddle.
(Photo by the author.)

Peter Paniddle.
(Photo by the author.)

A Kollection of Kiddles frolic in the **Liddle Kiddles Talking Townhouse.**
Top Row: (L to R) **Loretta and Luanna Locket, Liddle Middle Muffet,** and **Liddle Biddle Peep.**
Bottom Row: (L to R) **Shirley Skediddle, Liddle Diddle** and **Sizzly Friddle.**

RELATED COLLECTIBLES

Other items of interest to Kiddle collectors are:

Liddle Kiddles Let's Go Fishin' Game: A card game with a picture of Lola Liddle in a fishing boat on the front. This and the following three games all came in lunchbox-style plastic boxes with handles.

Liddle Kiddles Riddle Game: A matching game featuring four Kiddles on the front.

Liddle Kiddles Color Bingo Game: A bingo game using different colored pennies instead of numbers, and featuring Florence Niddle on the cover.

Liddle Kiddle Baby Animals Game: A game matching "Mother" cards to "Baby" cards, featuring Liddle Diddle on the front.

Kiddle Kases: Sleeping Biddle's castle, Cinderiddle's Palace, Alice's Castle, Kiddles Talking Townhouse, and the Liddle Kiddles Klub House to name a few. Storybook castles can fetch up to $80.00 in mint condition.

Liddle Kiddles wallet: Shows Surfy and Freezy on the front.

Kiddle Koloring books and paper doll sets

Skediddle Kiddle Popup Town: A Kiddle Kommunity with a large play yard.

Clockwise from center: **Funny Bunny**, **Violet Kologne**, **Bluebell Kologne**, two **Santa Kiddles**, **Honeysuckle Kologne**, and **Lucious Lime Kola Kiddle** (glitter variation).

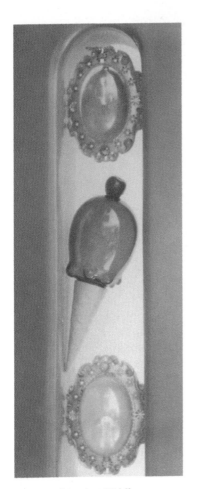

Kone and Locket Kiddle Kontainers. *(Photo by the author.)*

Mini-Kiddle Popup Playhouses: Tiny playsettings designed for the small, Locket-sized Kiddles.

Kiddle Kolony: A large three-room playhouse for Kiddles with a staircase and a sun deck.

Playhouse Kiddles: Individual rooms that could be stacked on top of each other to form a doll house. Each room came with furniture and its own Kiddle. Good-Night Kiddle, wearing a ruffly nightgown, came in a hot pink and purple bedroom; Pretty-Parlor Kiddle, a blonde wearing an orange and green dress and apron came in an orange and yellow living room; and Cookin' Kiddle, a brunette wearing a pink and blue dress, came in a yellow kitchen.

Snap-Happy Furniture sets: These were made from the same molds as the Playhouse Furniture sets, but came in different colors. The living room is red, white and blue; the bedroom is yellow; but the kitchen remains the same yellow as the Playhouse set. There was also a green and orange patio set.

Liddle Kiddle Toy Totes: Little luggage to tote around Kiddles and accessories. Produced were an overnight case with Calamity and Bunson on the front, a hatbox with Lola and Biff on the front and a traincase with Calamity and Bunson on the front.

Liddle Kiddles Electric Drawing Desk

Liddle Kiddle Frame-Tray Puzzles

Kiddle Komedy Threatre: A playset which included larger-than-Kiddle sized puppets that operated with swivel stix, a stage with two back drops, a record, and four masks.

Liddle Kiddle Trace and Color Sets

Liddle Kiddle 3-D postcard: Available from the 1970 Expo in Japan. The Kiddles are riding in a hot air balloon and are dressed in ethnic costumes representing various countries from around the world. The words "EXPO 70" are in the lower left hand corner.

Liddle Kiddle Viewmaster Reels

Liddle Kiddle Telephone Records: Tiny black records that inserted into the Mattel-O-Phone, manufactured in 1965. The Kiddles record is marked Mattel Inc. 1964 4830-205 Telephone. The inside circular label shows a picture of four Kiddles and reads "Liddle Kiddles/1965 Mattel Inc."

Chitty Chitty Bank Bank Kiddles: A special gift set which included four Kiddles to commemorate four of the characters from the movie.

Liddle Kiddle Lunchbox and Thermos kits

Liddle Kiddles captured the hearts and imaginations of an entire generation. There have been many baby dolls over the years, many 11$\frac{1}{2}$-inch fashion dolls, and many eight-inch toddler dolls. The Liddle Kiddle dolls' size and playful personalities make them singular and unique in the arena of dolls and they seem to be increasing in collectibility each year.

Babe Biddle.

SONGS CHILDREN LOVE

Rarer than rare is this children's record album of Bible songs that used Kiddles on the front and back of its jacket. Produced by Singcord Corp. for Zondervan, it seems as though the use of the Kiddles for the cover was probably unlicensed. I have heard of only three in the hands of collectors.

Songs Children Love
record album.

Liddle Kiddles Spanish Sticker Book.
(Photo courtesy of Linda Strumski.)

Color Variation Jewelry Treasure Box.
(Photo courtesy of Linda Strumski.)

LIDDLE KIDDLES SPANISH STICKER BOOK

This Spanish version sticker book falls into the "rarer than rare" category. Many collectors have never even heard of it. It was published by a company called "Novaro."

COLOR VARIATION JEWELRY TREASURE BOX

Extremely rare is this variation of the "Jewelry Kiddles Treasure Box"—essentially a jewelry storage case which opens up to tiny compartments for the Jewelry Kiddles. These Treasure Boxes were exclusively found in a red version (stock #3735). Collectors know of only one of the above (stock #5166). The front of this box pictures all of the Kiddles in their cases, and the colors used are yellow in the center and orange along the border, with green inside.

LIDDLE KIDDLES LUNCHBOX AND THERMOS KIT

Very hard to find and very pricey is this Thermos-brand lunchbox and thermos set which features Lemons Stiddle, Slipsy Sliddle and Kampy Kiddle. The lunchbox is a vinyl material with a white handle.

Liddle Kiddles Lunchbox and Thermos Kit.
(Photo courtesy of Jill Salerno.)

Beat-A-Diddle

Beat-A-Diddle was a 1967 Sears Exclusive that is very hard to come by today and very pricey. A tiny rock star, she normally came dressed in a black background/floral print midriff top and bell bottom pants, with a brown and yellow flowered guitar and a microphone (the top of which was just like Barbie's SOLO IN THE SPOTLIGHT mike). She had the same face as Lola Liddle, a more common Kiddle, but with blue eyes instead of brown. An even rarer variation is the same doll in a red print, rather than the black print two-piece outfit pictured. (Note: the red outfit pictured here is not original.) The photo displayed here was submitted anonymously. It shows four Beat-A-Diddles, one with a mysterious shade of red hair. Among Kiddle collectors, no one can explain, at this point, where this redhead may have come from.

Beat-A-Diddle in Red

Here is the extremely rare variation of the Beat-A-Diddle doll, wearing a red, rather than the usual black print two-piece outfit. The Beat-A-Diddle Kiddles are rare to begin with, and this small distinction in the outfit's color makes her a true challenge to unearth, and a tremendous find for the collector!

Beat-A-Diddle in Red.
(Photo courtesy of Linda Strumski.)

Rolly Twiddle, the only Black Kiddle. *(Photo courtesy of Linda Strumski.)*

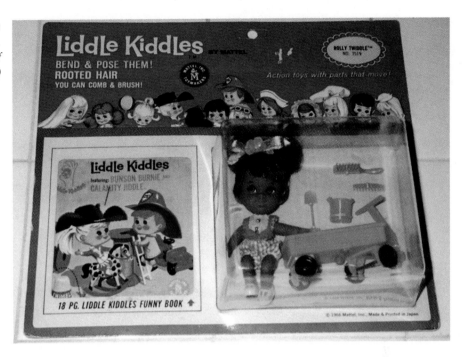

Liddle Kiddles Press-Out Book. *(Photo courtesy of Linda Strumski.)*

Lucky Locket coloring book, stock #1077. *(Photo courtesy of Linda Strumski.)*

ROLLY TWIDDLE

Another very rare item is the only Black Kiddle, Rolly Twiddle. She came with a pink and orange wagon, and the same pail and shovel as Millie Middle, only in orange instead of pink. She wore a green and white checked sunsuit and wore her hair up in a bun with a green ribbon. An even rarer Rolly Twiddle variation was owned by the late A. Glenn Offield. She had a middle part with four pigtails and no sidecurls.

LIDDLE KIDDLES PRESS-OUT BOOK

Extremely rare is this Whitman Press-out book (#1934), which included thirteen dolls and accessories. The set sold originally for 29 cents.

COLORING BOOKS

All collectors love finding paraphernalia related to the dolls they loved as a child. Coloring books are rarely found in untouched condition, and this Lucky Locket book, stock #1077, is a real find. Printed by Whitman, it originally sold for 39 cents, and like so many of the other Kiddle's paper play things, includes some very enjoyable Kiddle photography on its cover.

LIDDLE KIDDLES PLAY FUN SET

This is another set that very few collectors own, or have even had the opportunity to lay eyes on. It included a large sheet that the child was supposed to color in and use as the backdrop for a set of punchouts that were replicas of Kiddles and their accessories.

Liddle Kiddles Play Fun Set.
(Photo courtesy of Linda Strumski.)

SKEDIDDLE KIDDLE STICKER PICTURES

As in the case of most disposable paper products, this sticker book—which features a great cover shot of the Skediddle Kiddles—is very hard to come by.

Skediddle Kiddle Sticker Pictures.
(Photo courtesy of Linda Strumski.)

TREASURE TRIO

Extremely hard to find, especially NRFB (never removed from box) is this Jewelry Kiddles Treasure Trio Set featuring flower theme locket dolls.

Treasure Trio.
(Photo courtesy of Linda Strumski.)

LIDDLE KIDDLES TOWN

Very hard to find is this powder blue suitcase arrangement that opens into an entire Kiddle Kommunity.

Liddle Kiddles Town.
(Photo courtesy of Linda Strumski.)

Cinderiddle's Palace.

Baby Liddle.
(Photo courtesy of Linda Strumski.)

CINDERIDDLE'S PALACE

Hard to find MOC (mint on card) is Cinderirddle and her Palace, which includes both her ball gown and her tatters and a broom. This particular little doll has a side-part variation.

BABY LIDDLE

Here is Baby Liddle, a tiny snippet of a baby doll, that gets a huge reaction out of collectors. A Sears exclusive, she was made for a limited time and is currently hard to find, despite the larger number of seekers.

LIDDLE KIDDLES MAGIC SLATE

In speaking with collectors, this magic slate made by Whitman seems to be extremely rare.

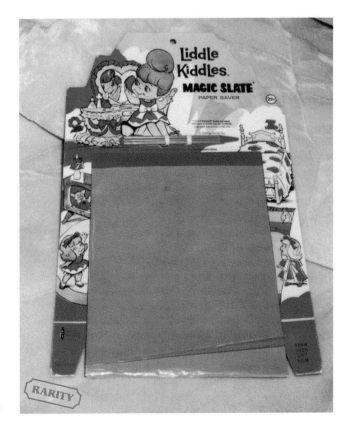

Liddle Kiddles Magic Slate.
(Photo courtesy of Linda Strumski.)

Zoolery Kiddles.
(Photo courtesy of Linda Strumski.)

ZOOLERY KIDDLES

These four Zoolery Kiddles: Playful Panther (yellow cage); Little Lion (purple cage); Chummy Chimp (blue cage); and Brawny Bear (green cage) are considered hard to find.

ALICE IN WONDERLIDDLE'S CASTLE

Even harder to find MOC is Alice, in her classic blue and white pinafore with her rabbit friend and his watch, and outfitted by a castle that opens up for many hours of imaginative play. This castle is significantly larger than Cinderiddle's Palace.

Alice in Wonderliddle's Castle.
(Photo courtesy of Linda Strumski.)

HAIRSTYLE VARIATIONS

Another unexplained variation is this Liddle Biddle Peep with factory braided hair. Liddle Biddle Peep was made with three ringlets that were tied back in a ponytail. The original owner of this doll remembers buying her at a store in her neighborhood in Alabama when she was a child, with this hairdo. She is shown here next to a Liddle Middle Muffet who commonly has this braided hairstyle to show that the two "do's" are identical. It's not at all likely that a child could have undone the original ringlets and braided Liddle Biddle Peep's hair so perfectly. What appears to be the original rubber band is at the bottom of the braid. So far, this doll is one-of-a kind. It would be fun to find others that may be out there!

Two different views of Liddle Biddle Peep.
(Dolls provided by Terry Carter. Photo courtesy of Patti Cooke.)

OTHER RARE KIDDLE ITEMS

Liddle Kiddle Wallet

Extremely rare. Features Surfy and Freezy on the front. The original stock number is 5050, and the author reports knowing only two advanced collectors who own one.

Frame Tray Puzzles

All varieties are rare, but especially the Storybook Puzzles featuring photography of Liddle Middle Muffet, Sleeping Biddle, Red Riuding Hiddle and Cinderiddle. (Point of interest: the Cinderiddle puzzle depicts her in both her ball gown and tatters, but it is actually Kampy Kiddle who is modeling the tatters—there must have been some clause in Cinderiddle's contract. You know what fame can do to one's head!)

Little Kiddle
Electric Drawing Desk

3-D postcard

Extremely rare, it was sold at the 1970 EXPO in Japan. Nine Kiddles, each in a different ethnic costume, are shown flying high over the earth in a hot air balloon. Like the album cover, this picture may have been unlicensed, as there is no mention of "Kiddles" or "Mattel" anywhere on the card.

Liddle Kiddle
Trace and Color Set

The set description read: "Trace parts of two pictures to make a third picture."

◆ Some Animiddle Kiddles were packaged in Whitman Candy boxes, along with the chocolates. Finding one in its original box (without the candy, of course) is a truly rare find, as very few people thought to save the candy box!

TERRI LEE RARITIES

So lovingly fond of her daughter, Terri Lee, was Mrs. Violet Gradwohl that she spent years designing a carefully engineered doll in her likeness. Because Mrs. Gradwohl had seen her daughter break down in tears on more than one occasion over a broken doll, she wanted to create and manufacture a doll with her daughter's name that was especially durable—maybe even unbreakable—with eyes that wouldn't fall out and hair that would remain intact. She began an avid search for a type of plastic that would withstand the rigor of child's play, and developed a style of doll's eyes that were actually molded into the head itself. The wigs she chose for these dolls were also of high quality and durable, could be set and shampooed, and were the first doll wigs ever to have a lifetime guarantee. What followed, naturally, was a wardrobe of exceptional design and workmanship, and the end result was pure Quality. To her many fans, the name Terri Lee is synonymous with "quality."

Terri Lee dolls began to be manufactured in August of 1946 out of a single room in Lincoln, Nebraska. Offering a

Vinyl **Jerri and Terri Lee's** wearing beautiful mint Sunflower Outfits.
(Photo courtesy of Sue Munsell.)

Standard **Terri Lee's** in Roller Skating Outfits. *(Photos courtesy of Sue Munsell.)*

Terri, Jerri, Tiny Terri and **Tiny Jerri** in Majorette Outfits. *(Photo courtesy of Sue Munsell.)*

lifetime guarantee and a hospital for "sick Terri Lee dolls," they were well received from the start. A monthly magazine filled with patterns, contests, and fun activities was sent to each Terri Lee owner. In time, Terri Lee had a brother, Jerri. Mrs. Gradwohl felt that the black children of America would enjoy having dolls in their likeness as well, and thus came Bonnie Lu and Benje (and later, Patty Jo, based on a popular comic character). Following in the years to come were Nanook, an Eskimo child; Tiny Terri; Tiny Jerri; Baby Linda, an eleven-inch soft vinyl meant to be a baby's first doll; and Connie Lynn, a larger version at twenty inches. All of these dolls, except Baby Linda and Connie Lynn, had the same bodies (marked TERRI LEE) but had variations in hair and skin coloring. Eventually, the Terri Lee dolls featured sleep eyes.

Terri Lee in her Frontier
Outfit with coonskin cap.
(Photo courtesy of Sue Munsell)

The unique nature of Terri Lee dolls created a lot of interest among the American public and the media. They were featured on television and in movie shorts, and were written up in several national publications aimed at both children and adults. Black periodicals such as the N*egro* D*igest* and E*bony* commended her efforts. In many ways, these dolls broke ground and set new standards. Within five years of its humble beginnings, the Terri Lee Doll Company was selling in excess of 3,000 dolls per week, and had more business than it could handle.

A factory fire during the Christmas season of 1951 that was not completely covered by insurance slowed down future production considerably, and the fever pitch of the doll's hey day was never reached again.

These dolls have a distinctive look to them that no one seems to have successfully imitated, with a rather flat mid face, and very large, prominent dark eyes with a sort of "made up" look to them.

Terri Lee dolls in Scotty Outfits, (left) with a painted **Terri Lee** on the left; **Terri** and **Tiny Terri** (right) in matching spring suits with wheat pattern.
(Photos courtesy of Sue Munsell.)

Terri Lee Ferris Wheel.
(Photo courtesy of Sandy Dorsey.)

TERRI LEE FERRIS WHEEL

Manufactured by the W.I. Stensgaard Company of Chicago around 1956, this motorized Ferris Wheel was designed to hold twelve Tiny Terri Lees, each in their own individual stands, and was offered to stores carrying Terri Lee Dolls for $75. This had to be a very effective tool in catching the eyes of many a young shopper, as it revolved an adorable parade of these miniature Terri Lee dolls. Terri Lee collectors consulted know of only three of these Ferris Wheels in existence.

Additional photos of the **Ferris Wheel.** The actual measurements of the Ferris Wheel are 50-inches high and eighteen-inches across the front of base. *(Photos courtesy of Dorene Reed.)*

Patty Jo, (left) and **Benji** (right) are two more examples of the Black Terri Lee dolls. This Benji is considered a "painted" Terri Lee because he is made of a new plastic material that the company used—actually a greenish material which was then painted over in either typical flesh tone or in a medium brown for the Black dolls. *(Photo courtesy of Sandy Dorsey.)*

BLACK TERRI LEE

Whether these dolls started out as Bonnie Lu's, Benji's or Patty Jo's, they are known collectively as Black Teri Lee's and are considered rare on today's collector's market.

Black Terri Lee.
(Photo courtesy of Pat Rather.)

Bonnie Lou, Composition Terri Lee.
(Photo courtesy of Sandy Dorsey.)

COMPOSITION TERRI LEE

The very first Terri Lee dolls manufactured were of composition, a rather organic material using—frequently—flour, water, sawdust, glue, and sometimes straw. These dolls were produced before the company converted over to hard plastic. Here is a Black composition Bonnie Lou, probably made between 1946 and 1947. As with all composition dolls, she will eventually meet with some heart-breaking cracking and crazing.

HISPANIC TERRI LEES

How ahead of her time was Mrs. Gradwohl! Not only Black versions, but also Hispanic versions of Teri Lee dolls were created. With dramatic coloring and striking features, these dolls with their incredibly beautiful black hair are rare and highly sought after by collectors.

Hispanic Terri Lees.
(Photos courtesy of Sandy Dorsey.)

Two examples of this precious version of the Terri Lee doll, both the large and small version of **Alice in Wonderland.**
(Photo courtesy of Sandy Dorsey.)

THE TERRI LEE
ALICE IN WONDERLAND DOLL

Another rare and sought after issue. In classic Alice in Wonderland-style pinafore dresses, these dolls have a special appeal to collectors. The dresses are said to have come in silvery blue, light blue and light pink.

Two **Alice in Wonderland Terri Lees.**
(Photo courtesy of Pat Rather.)

THE GENE AUTRY DOLL

Said to be a good friend of the Gradwohl family, Gene Autry, popular Western star of the time, was immortalized in doll form. He appears to have the same head mold as the other Terri Lee dolls, but with different face painting. He is sixteen-inches tall, all hard plastic, and very hard to find today, even in Terri Lee collector circles.

VINYL TERRI AND JERRI LEES

The very earliest of the Terri Lee dolls were made of composition, while Mrs. Gradwohl continued her lengthy search for the "unbreakable" medium she longed for. Once she found it, almost all of the Terri Lee dolls, with the exception of Baby Linda, were made of hard plastic. No one seems to know the origins of these vinyl Terri and Jerri Lees. Many speculate that it was simply an experiment.

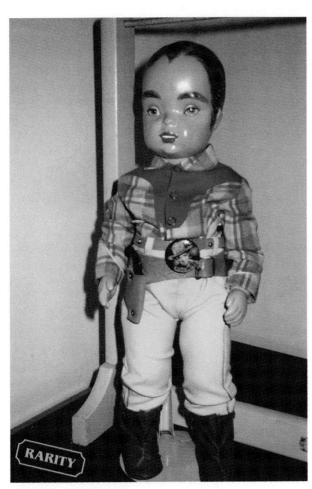

The Gene Autry Doll.
(Photo courtesy of Pat Rather.)

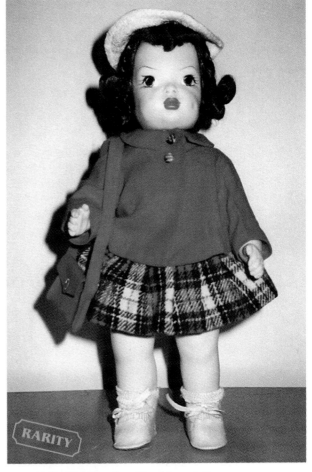

One of the vinyl Terri and Jerri Lee dolls.
(Photo courtesy of Pat Rather.)

RARITY

Talking Terri Lee.
*(Photo courtesy
of Sandy Dorsey.)*

Close up detail of the
Talking Terri Lee.
*(Photo courtesy of
Sandy Dorsey.)*

TALKING TERRI LEE

Somewhat easy to find in the state of California, but more difficult for the rest of the country, is this Talking Terri Lee doll, complete with records, cord and complete outfit. In her time, she was referred to as "The National Baby Sitter." She could sing and tell stories, by virtue of a speaker and jack arrangement in her head. A cord connected the jack in the doll's head to any available record player. Special records, "Terri Tales," and "Terri Tunes" were made for her and she came with a warning to keep her away from water. Some of the later dolls had the jack in the back of the head but did not have speakers. The Talking Terri Lees all had speakers!

What a sensation she must have created for the wide-eyed children of the 1950s, many of whom had never even dreamed of a doll that could talk to them!

Collector's Advisory

Please remember that the Terri Lee Company continued to use the "jack head" in some of the later dolls, but did not include the speaker. Perhaps the Talking Terri Lees did not sell as well as originally forecast and, like Mattel, the company wanted to use up the extra parts. To be a Talking Terri Lee doll, she must have both the jack AND the speaker perforations in the head. Also, please remember that she is hard to find with her complete set up—which includes the records, cord and adapter!

Terri Lee Steiff Monkeys. Finding these little cuties completely dressed is the real trick. Pictured here are both the boy and the girl, in complete outfits. *(Photo courtesy of Sandy Dorsey.)*

TERRI LEE STEIFF MONKEYS

Some of the Terri Lee and Jerri Lee outfits came with stuffed Steiff animals.

TERRI LEE WALKER

Hard to find is this Terri Lee Walker doll, made with holes in her feet which fit perfectly into her special red push cart. When pushed, the cart caused the doll to make walking movements.

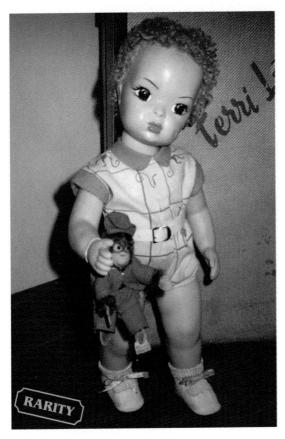

Pictured is **Jerri Lee** with his pet monkey "Tony." *(Photo courtesy of Pat Rather.)*

Pig-Tailed Terri Lee.
(Photo courtesy of Sue Munsell.)

Terri Lee Walker.
(Photo courtesy of Lynn Artel.)

Pig-Tailed Terri Lee

This rare hairstyle variation is adorable on Terri Lee, pictured here with Jerri Lee in their wool spring coats and straw hats. This variation is only considered rare if the doll has jet black hair.

Snobby Poodle

Another of the Terri Lee pets, this darling pooch in his red and gold doggie coat is considered hard to find. Tending him here is Terri Lee in her square-dancing outfit.

Terri Lee and Snobby Poodle.
(Photo courtesy of Sue Munsell.)

This is the **Tole Painted Deluxe Wardrobe** made for Terri Lee, which was hand painted over the natural wood grain, and featured her initials. *(Photo courtesy of Sandy Dorsey.)*

Small winter wardrobe (left) and a large **Deluxe Wardrobe** (right). *(Photo courtesy of Pat Rather.)*

TERRI LEE WARDROBES

Several wardrobes were manufactured for the Terri Lee dolls. In today's market they are extremely hard to come by. Pictured are a small winter wardrobe and a large Deluxe Wardrobe.

TERRI LEE LAMPS

This item is so rare that many collectors have never even heard of one. This example shows a picture of a Terri Lee doll dressed in her Sunday best, with the inscription "Love, Terri Lee."

OTHER TERRI LEE ITEMS

Other hard-to-find Terri Lee items would include the Terri Lee Hair Dress Kit, a small cardboard box with comb, brush, curlers and shampoo, sometimes barrettes and a hair net; Linda's Musical Bassinette and Tree, a wooden tree with an extra long limb from which a frilly cradle was suspended—played "Rock-A-Bye-Baby"; the Tiny Terri Lee Bridal Cedar Chest, which was a miniature Lane Hope Chest with bridal and trousseau wear; and past issues of the *Terri Lee Magazine*.

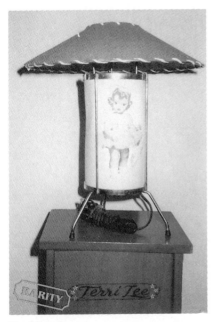

Terri Lee Lamp.
(Photo courtesy of Pat Rather.)

GINNETTE RARITIES

In the mid-1950s, the Vogue Company introduced both an older and a younger sister for their little leading lady, Ginny. Jill, the older sister, was a 10½-inch hard plastic teen doll with high-heeled feet. And Ginnette, Ginny's little sister, was a precious eight-inch all vinyl baby doll, with a winsome little face and meticulously detailed hands and feet. She had painted blue eyes, molded hair, and was marked "Vogue Dolls, Inc." on her middle back. She also had a tiny poppy red nurser mouth and could drink and wet. So many small, vinyl, drink-and-wet babies sprang up in the late '50s and early '60s that today Ginnette looks like one of the crowd, and is frequently not distinguished as a hot collectible. She is, therefore, often found in bargain bins and in tiny corners of antique malls with tiny price tags to match. But you and I know her as Ginny's little sister and realize how special she is.

(Photo courtesy Shari Ogilvie Collection.)

71

"Jimmy." *(Photo courtesy Shari Ogilvie Collection.)*

(Photo by the author.)

Like Ginny and Jill, Ginnette had an array of outfits, accessories and even furniture. A 1958 Christmas catalog shows Ginnette in a small print diaper and with a baby bottle for a price of $3. This is the basic Ginnette doll, first introduced in 1955. She originally came with a circular wrist tag that read, "Hi! I'm Ginnette." Her glass bottle held a tiny paper label with her picture on it. During this first year of production, Ginnette had only five outfits. But at the time of this Christmas catalog, three years later, a host of new outfits, including a white felt coat and matching bonnet, sun dress, and hooded snowsuit were selling for between $1.50 and $2.50. Ginnette's baby pack, with extra diapers, bottle and layette, sold for $6. Additional outfits through the years included beautiful organdy dresses with lace and ribbon trim and matching bonnets, classic christening gowns, and several outfits that matched both Ginny's and those of her eventual little brother, Jimmy. (The way to tell Ginnette and Jimmy dolls apart, incidentally, is to note that Ginnette had painted eyelashes and Jimmy had none). Ginnette's clothing was always fastened with either ties or hooks and eyes. All of Ginnette's clothing is decidedly well made, especially by today's standards, with special attention given to the choice of materials and trims. Most, but not all, of her outfits were tagged "VOGUE DOLLS, INC./MEDFORD, MASS. U.S.A./REG. PAT OFF." Among Ginnette's accessories were rattles, a bathinette, a crib, a baby tender, a wading pool, bedroom furniture, bedding sets, bath sets and even a personalized necklace.

As the years passed, Ginnette herself changed in some ways. In 1956 she had sleep eyes; in 1963 she had rooted hair; and in 1957 she could cry real tears, in addition to drinking and wetting. In 1959, she was available in both painted-eye and sleep-eye versions. Both sleep-eye and painted-eye Ginnettes were made with "cooing" devices, but the devices used in the sleep-eye dolls seem to have held up better over the years.

Ginnette had consistently remained eight-inches tall until 1985 when she was produced as both a nine-inch vinyl baby doll with sleep eyes and rooted hair, and as a special edition porcelain christening doll with very detailed sculpted hair.

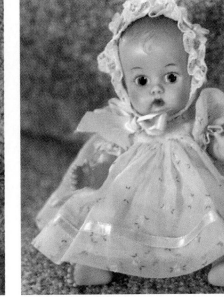

(Dolls and photographs courtesy of Shari Ogilvie.)

Let's keep our fingers crossed to see if there will be a new Baby Ginnette born in this decade who can, perhaps, recapture the charm she has thus far always emanated. Because it was the wish of Jenny Graves, Ginny's creator, that her dolls never be advertised on television, they have never been as hugely popular as Barbie or Cabbage Patches. But to her many fans, Baby Ginnette will always be "In Vogue."

THE BLACK GINNETTE

Like many Black dolls within a series, the Black Ginnette was made in limited numbers and is now hard to find.

The Black Ginnette.
(Doll and photograph courtesy of Shari Ogilvie.)

Additional rare **Black Ginnettes.** The Ginnette on the right with the molded hair is from about 1958 and wears outfit #2361. The Ginnette on the left with the rooted hair is wearing an unknown outfit. *(Photo courtesy of Rhonda Schoenick.)*

Jimmy Cowboy

Considered rare is this dressed version of Jimmy, which sold originally in 1958 for $2.50. It includes blue denim coveralls, red jersey shirt, black cowboy hat, red shoes and a silver toned pistol. Too cute for words! The outfit could also be purchased separately, without the doll.

Jimmy Cowboy.
(Photo and doll courtesy of Shari Ogilvie.)

Jimmy Clown.
(Photo and doll courtesy of Shari Ogilvie.)

Jimmy Clown

Another 1958 rarity for Jimmy was the clown ensemble. Pink on one side, blue on the other, it had white pompons in the center and came with one blue and one pink shoe and a matching cap. The outfit could be purchased on or off the Jimmy doll and originally sold for $2.50, a tiny fraction of what it is worth today.

Ginnette's Red Shoes

Like two tiny hen's teeth, Ginnette collectors will tell you how hard it is to find this pair of shoes for Ginnette. Shown here Mint in Box, packaged with a pair of socks, this set came in a pink and blue print box and is a coveted find for today's collector.

THE GINNETTE CRYER

You may own what you think is a garden variety sleep-eye Ginnette, and not realize that she is a very hard to find Ginnette Cryer. The way to determine the difference is to carefully remove her precious little head and count the number of tubes leading from the body to the head of the doll. A standard nursing Ginnette will have only one tube which leads from the mouth to the body, but a crying Ginnette will have three (usually red) tubes, including one for each eye. Her box reads "7678 -TEARING EYE DOLL - $4.00" and she came with an instruction sheet titled "I'm Ginnette - How to Make Me Cry."

Ginnette's Red Shoes.
(Photo and doll accessory courtesy of Shari Ogilvie.)

GINNETTE CHEST OF DRAWERS

Another very hard to find and highly sought-after item in the realm of Ginnette collectibles is this wooden chest of drawers personalized with her name.

The Ginnette Cryer. *(Doll and photo courtesy of Shari Ogilvie.)*

Ginnette Chest of Drawers.
(Photo courtesy of Lynn Artel.)

Brown-Eyed Jill.
(Photo courtesy of Tina Ritari.)

JILL RARITIES

In 1957, Vogue Dolls, Inc. added to their family tree by introducing an older sister for their bright star, Ginny. Jill, as she was called, was a 10$\frac{1}{2}$-inch hard plastic teenage doll with a younger look and personality than the Mattel Barbie doll that followed her two years later. She is precious, and her clothes are very well made and accessorized—but she never became a big seller. There were many of this type of teenage doll in that era, and none of them stood out enough to become hugely popular. Like Ginnette herself, she too can be lost in that same crowd today as, undressed, she looks like one of the "generics" of the late '50s. So many flea market and antique dealers today concentrate so heavily on Barbie that dolls like Jill can be buried in piles on bargain tables, just waiting to be unearthed by a collector in the know. How can one tell her from the tons of other ten inchers? She is marked "VOGUE" on the back of her neck and "JILL VOGUE DOLLS INC. MADE IN USA c 1957" on her back. Remember, to doll lovers, all Vogue dolls are collectible!

The standard Jill doll came as a blonde, brunette or redhead, in either a short bob with bangs or a ponytail. As with all hard plastic dolls, her wigs were glued on, and in Jill's case consumers could buy replacement wigs for her. She had blue sleep eyes with molded lashes, red lipstick and nail polish, and pink cheek blush.

The basic Jill doll usually came in a mint green box with a fold-over lid and sold originally for $3. Her clothing is beautifully made, using top quality fabrics which include real furs and leathers, and is tagged "Vogue Dolls, Inc." Some of her outfits matched Ginny's and even Ginnette's, and tiny accessories such as charm bracelets and headbands could be purchased separately.

In 1958, Vogue gave Jill a best friend—Jan—who is today most frequently confused with Jill. To set the record straight, Jan was made of rigid vinyl, rather than hard plastic, and is only marked "VOGUE" on her neck.

The race with the increasingly popular Barbie was a tough one, and the Jan and Jill dolls finally ran out of gas in 1965, when they were discontinued. Over the years, they have always been well received by those who loved them and they make a wonderful addition to a doll collection today because, like so many Vogue dolls, they are a tribute to the standards of quality of a bygone era.

BROWN-EYED JILL

This unusual variation in eye color makes Jill a real collectors' find.

Flip-Haired Jill.
(Photo courtesy of Tina Ritari.)

FLIP-HAIRED JILL

This pretty blonde sports a rare variation in hairstyles for Jill. Her standard style was either a bob (called "Angel cut") or a ponytail. As you can see, Vogue always used a generous amount of top quality saran.

JILL DRESSED DOLL IN BOX

Like the dressed Barbies, the dressed Jills were sold in boxes that were labeled with a stock number that corresponded to the stock number of the outfit that the doll was dressed in. These dressed dolls were sold in boxes that resembled Ginny boxes, but were a minty green, instead of the Ginny pink. Very hard to find.

Collector's Advisory

Because of the hardness of the plastic used for hard plastic dolls, their hair could not be rooted as a vinyl doll's could. This has made the practice of replacing wigs rather common, as the wigs can simply be torn off and a new one glued on. In the case of this rare flip variation, this is a particular concern. Become familiar with what the original Jill Flip wig looks like, and with the texture and general feel of Jill hair in general. These qualities would be hard to imitate. Also, check for any glue reside at the hairline.

Almost all of Jill's clothing is fastened with snaps that read "Dot Starlet" on the underside, and they are usually tagged "Vogue Dolls, Inc." If there is any concern about reproduction clothing, look for these very distinctive snaps. Tags, of course, can fall out over the years, but it seems that quite a few of Vogue's tags have remained intact.

ADDITIONAL JILL RARITIES

◆ The Jill Teen Togs Gift Set

◆ Jill Charm Bracelet

◆ Jill Watch

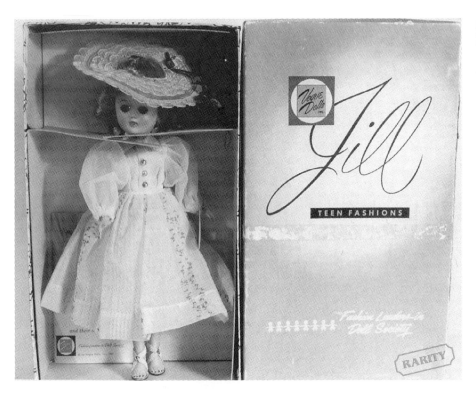

Jill Dressed Doll in Box.
(Photo courtesy of Tina Ritari.)

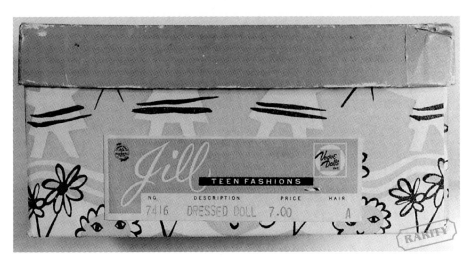

Side view of **Jill Dressed Doll Box.**
(Photo courtesy of Tina Ritari.)

RARITY

Vicki Tuttell's Helen Blue,
"Courtney Erin."

80

Cabbage Patch Rarities

In 1982, Coleco secured the rights to Xavier Robert's "Little People," a line of soft-sculpture dolls with meek and unpretentious personas, made at a most unique doll hospital called Babyland General near Helen, Georgia. These engaging little pixies started lining the store shelves by June of '83, with their faces that only a mother could love and their humble little eyes that seemed to implore "Pick me up." The public's reaction to them, at first, was lukewarm. By August, many of them started to go on clearance. Somehow, as the Christmas season of 1983 approached, their novel looks and personalities must have started to grow on people, because sales started to pick up. By Christmas Day, 2.5 million of them had sold and the factory was working overtime trying to keep up with the demand. Parents and collectors stood in line at stores that were thought to be getting a shipment of these dolls. Store clerks tossed Cabbage Patch boxes into noisy crowds that had congregated by stockroom doors, jumping and grabbing like bridesmaids for a bouquet. Some dolls even came to stores in armored cars, and in such small qualities that they had to be auctioned off, one at a time. Never had any doll so captured the undivided attention of both the public and the media.

The first Cabbage Patch Kids by Coleco are marked "COPY R. 1978 1982/ORIGINAL APPALACHIAN ART WORKS INC./MANUFACTURED BY COLECO IND. INC." on their heads and have the stamped signature of Xavier Robers on their rear ends. The signature colors varied from year to year as follows:

1984	Green
1985	Aqua
1986	Red
1987	Aqua again
1988	Purple
1989	Watermelon

After this year, Hasbro took over production of the Cabbage Patch dolls. Over the years, the variety of types and the variations within those types has been tremendous—more than with any other modern doll. Babies, Preemies, Splashin' Kids, Talking Kids, Cornsilk Kids with nylon as opposed to yarn hair, Farm Babies, Twins, Baseball Kids and Clowns, are just a few of the many categories. And, within those categories there are over twenty different faces; a tremendous variety of hair colors and styles, including Baldies; some dolls with dimples, and some with teeth; some with pacifiers; some boys and some girls; some with blue eyes, some with brown . . . and so on. Cabbage Patch collectors probably have more fun than the rest of us. I imagine that they could accumulate quite a collection without ever having two that are alike!

CABBAGE PATCH RARITIES

"Little People" was the name of the very first soft-sculpture dolls made by Xavier Robers at Babyland General in Georgia, and they were the forerunners to the famous Cabbage Patch Kids. Many of these dolls, which were made in limited numbers to begin with, were played with and some were even given away to church rummage sales and the like, as it would have taken the wisdom of Solomon to have guessed at their eventual value. The fact that many of these early dolls were discarded or destroyed adds to their rarity. The issue of the doll can usually be determined by the "birth certificates" furnished with them which gave much information such as dates and which were bordered in different colors. In the case of foreign-made Cabbage Patches, their body tags provide issue information. Dolls were either hand signed by Xavier Robers, or stamped, as noted. All values here are Averaged, as there is a considerable range in all Cabbage Patch pricing!

Helen Blue: These were the very first soft-sculpture dolls made in 1978 by Xavier Robers himself. Limited to 1,000 and with a real signature, these dolls are valued today at between $3,000 and $7,000. Research indicates that these prices are indeed being realized. The Helen Blue dolls had a blue birth certificate.

"A" Dolls: Immediately followed the Helen Blues. Also made during 1978; came with a blue birth certificate; limited to 1,000 issued, with a real signature, and valued at about $3,500 each.

"B" Dolls: Made during 1978 and 1979, with real signatures and red birth certificates, they were a limited issue of 1,000. These dolls are currently valued at around $3,000.

"C" Dolls: A higher percentage of these dolls have been found in played-with condition. Perhaps they were lower priced to begin with and more were purchased as playthings. Five thousand were made in 1979, and they came with real signatures and burgundy birth certificates. They are valued today at about $2,000.

"D" Dolls: Ten thousand of these dolls were made in 1979, with real signatures and purple birth certificates. They are currently valued at around $600.

"X" Christmas Dolls: These were the very first Christmas dolls made in the Cabbage Patch line. Limited to 15,000, they were made during 1979 and 1980, and are valued at around $750.

"E" Dolls: Also produced during 1979 and 1980, 15,000 of these dolls were made, with real signatures and bronze birth certificates, and they are valued at about $500.

1980 Special Preemie: These were the very first Preemie Dolls made in the Cabbage Patch line, and were limited to 5,000, with real signatures. They sell today for about $300.

1980 Celebrity Dolls: The cast of the television show, "Real People," visited Babyland General during this time frame, and special dolls were made and dressed for the taping. Five thousand dolls were created with red pants and tennis shoes and T-shirts that read "I'm a TV Celebrity." The dolls are valued today at about $400.

Nicholas and Noel: This 1980 Christmas set—a boy and a girl—were limited in production to 2,500 items, with real signatures. They sell today for about $2,000 for the set.

1980 Grand Edition: These dolls were 27-inches tall, with wire skeletons that allowed them to stand. The girls were dressed in minks and diamond earrings, and the boys were in tuxedos. Only 1,000 were made and they are valued today at about $1,500.

"U" Dolls: These were the first dolls to display the stamped signature. Some 73,000 of them were made during 1980. One would think that due to the stamped signature and the large production number, these dolls would have little value to collectors. As it turns out, however, these dolls were unusually attractive—chubbier and with beautiful heads of hair—so collectors loved them! They are valued at $400 each.

RARE COLECO
CABBAGE PATCH DOLLS

Boys with Red Shag Hair: These dolls came complete with freckles, they are valued at about $650. The 1983 issues had blue eyes, and the 1985-86 issues had green.

Black Dolls with Freckles: Found so far only on the #2 head mold, they are valued at about $700.

1983 Brown Fuzzy: These dolls had no loops in their hair, and had blue eyes and a pacifier. They are considered hard to find. Valued at about $150.

Hong Kong Dolls: The earliest Cabbage Patch dolls by Coleco were produced in Hong Kong. Their heads and body tags will indicate this. After about three million dolls were manufactured there, the Hong Kong factory was closed and the leftover Hong Kong heads were shipped to a new factory in China. These heads were then placed on bodies that were

Collector's Advisory

Find an advanced collector that you can trust, and experience first hand what the baby powder-scented Coleco Cabbage Patches smell like. This is the best way to help you make future determinations as to whether a doll has been factory scented or not. Be advised that there are colognes on the market that are baby powder scented and can be applied to a doll without the mess and fuss of the actual powder, and which leave no telltale signs.

For complete authenticity of the earliest dolls, check the tags on clothing and shoes! If they really belong on the doll, they will be marked with a factory code that will match the doll's body tag! The factory codes are either OK, KT or P.

tagged "Made in China." Therefore, dolls with Hong Kong heads and China bodies are common—dolls with both Hong Kong heads and bodies are considered rare.

Black #1 Head Mold: During the first year of Coleco's production, four different head molds were produced. The number of each head mold, 1, 2, 3, or 4, is imprinted on the back of the doll's head, right under the copyright. White dolls with the #1 head mold are common—black #1s are very hard to find.

Freckled #2s: Freckled dolls with the #2 head mold are scarce. The black freckled #2s are, of course, more rare, but even the white freckled #2s are sought after by collectors.

Small Eyed #3s: Most of the dolls with the #3 head mold have large eyes. The #3s with small eyes are considered harder to find.

Dark Brown Shag Boy with Blue Eyes: This combination among the early dolls is considered a rarity.

Auburn Single Ponytail Girl: First produced in 1983, and then again in 1987, she is also considered rare.

Baby Powder Scented Dolls: A very few of the early dolls have a distinct scent of baby powder, applied at the factory. This scent, when original, can add from 20 to 40 percent to a doll's value!

One-Toothed Brunette Side Ponytail with Blue Eyes: Produced in 1985, this little girl is considered by collectors to be extremely rare. Valued at about $350.

RARE FOREIGN-MADE CABBAGE PATCHES

As the demand for these dolls increased, factories all over the world began to help with the manufacturing. Listed below are very hard to find and very much sought after Cabbage Patches. Dolls can be identified by their body tags.

Tsukuda's 1983 Issue: Made in Japan through 1985, many of them are in Karate outfits and Oriental garb. Valued at about $100.

Lili Ledi Freckled Dolls: Made in Mexico during 1983. Valued at about $150.

Jesmar Dolls: Made in Spain in 1983. Body tag reads simply "J". Valued at about $100.

Triang Pedigree Dolls: Made in South Africa during 1983-85. Valued at about $100.

The **1983 Freckle-Faced Kids** are hard to find. *(Photo courtesy of Vicki Tuttell.)*

The **1983 Black Freckle Face** is a real rarity. *(Photo courtesy of Vicki Tuttell.)*

Helen Blue with Teddy Bear.
(Photo courtesy of Vicki Tuttell.)

HELEN BLUE

Here is one of the very first soft-sculpture "Little People" dolls hand made by Xavier Roberts. Little People are the predecessors to what we know today as the Cabbage Patch Kids. The first 1,000 dolls, made by the Original Appalachian Artworks Company at Babyland General, were made by Xavier himself without help from his mother or other employees. These initial 1,000 were called "Helen Blue's" after the town of Helen, Georgia, and the blue color of their birth certificates. The Helen Blues, made as both boys and girls in a variety of hair colors and styles, were made in 1978. They were dressed originally in garage sale clothing and sold for between $30 and $150. Today, they have their own line of designer clothing made specifically for them, and sell for between $3,000 and $7,000, depending on the area of the country. Many of the original Helen Blues were purchased as playthings, not investments, and because they have suffered the rigors of play, they have lost some of their value. Who could possibly have forecast the eventual empire these original dolls would build, the eventual hysteria that would sweep across the country as a result of their "birth," or their phenomenal increase in value over time?

Babyland General as it appears today in Cleveland, Georgia. *(Photo courtesy of Vicki Tuttell.)*

Courtney next to a
"C Burgundy" doll,
hand signed in 1979,
named **"Harlan Sean."**
*(Photo courtesy of
Vicki Tuttell.)*

Additional shot of
"Courtney Erin," the
Helen Blue owned
by Vicki Tuttell.
*(Photo courtesy
of Vicki Tuttell.)*

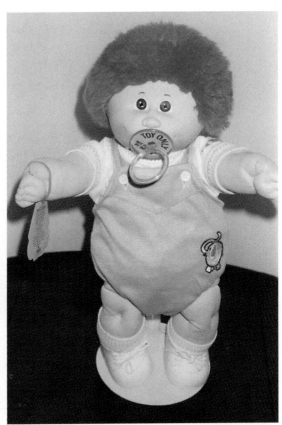

Two examples
of the rare
Red Shag Boy.
*(Photos
courtesy of
Marty Liston.)*

**Brown Side Ponytail with Blue Eyes and
One Tooth.** *(Photo courtesy of Marty Liston.)*

RED SHAG BOY

Two examples of the rare Red Shag Boy, (also called Red Fuzzy or Carrot Fuzzy), which appeared in 1983 with blue eyes, and later with green. The little guy on the left is wearing one of the rare early outfits: a powder blue knit romper with a duck appliqué (most had elephant appliqués). The squeezeable love bug on the right has a hard-to-find pacifier, which has large, dark letters.

BROWN SIDE PONYTAIL WITH BLUE EYES AND ONE TOOTH

Produced in 1985, this combination makes for a very rare doll, as most of these dolls were made with brown eyes.

JAPANESE BRIDE AND GROOM SET

Hard to find is this bride and groom set made in 1985 and exquisitely dressed. Also available was a bride in a pink dress. Value for the set is about $225.

Japanese Bride and Groom Set.
(Photo courtesy of Marty Liston.)

CORNSILK CABBAGE PATCH KIDS

In the late 1980s, Coleco introduced the adorable Cornsilk Cabbage Patch Kids, with nylon, rather than yarn, hair. This hard-to-resist little girl sports the rarest of the Cornsilk hairstyles, what collectors refer to as "Shirley Temple Curls". Her value is about $60, about five times the value of a typical Cornsilk Kid from this era.

Cornsilk Cabbage Patch Kid.
(Photo courtesy of Vicki Tuttell.)

LITTLE PEOPLE PALS

About 10,000 of these soft-sculpture originals were made in 1981 and '82, as playmates for the larger original kids. They had no individual papers, only tags on their outfits. A typical "Pal" is worth between $200-300. The tall and small boys on the left are prototypes, of which only 75 were made of each. Their value falls in the $800 range.

Little People Pals.
(Photo courtesy of Vicki Tuttell.)

1962 Tammy.
(Photo by the author.)

TAMMY RARITIES

Growing up in Skokie, Illinois, my next door neighbor, Linda, and I were ardent, dyed-in-the-wool Barbie fans. During summer vacations, we'd start as early as eight in the morning, and our miniature alter egos, with their bobbing ponytails, could host three parties, fly to New York and have seven serious arguments with their Kens before noon, when we reluctantly had to break for lunch. Like almost all of the other little girls in the country, Barbie was number one—the undisputed champion of boyfriends, parties and eyeliner. No other doll in the '60s was ever her equal, but one did come dangerously close.

First introduced in 1962 by the Ideal Toy Company, Tammy grabbed America's attention for one simple reason—she was not just another Barbie knock-off. She had a fresh, unique look and personality and could therefore stand on her own two feet. Tammy was an ingenue. She had a younger, more innocent look, with a more youthful figure and a far less sophisticated wardrobe. She was the "girl next door," and her sturdier build made her easier to handle and dress.

Standing twelve-inches tall, the early Tammys had thick glossy bobs that came in assorted shades of blonde. They are marked "Ideal Toy Corp/BS-12" on their heads, and "Ideal Toy Copr/BS-12/1" on their backs.

Her original outfits are of wonderful workmanship and quality, with much attention paid to detail, especially in the accessories.

In 1964, Pos'n Tammy was introduced—a bendable braided-hair version of the first Tammy. She had the same markings, except for a "BS-12/2" on her head.

The year 1965 brought Grown Up Tammy, ironically, ¼-inch shorter than the first two. Grown Up Tammy had a smaller head, a slimmer torso and a shorter pageboy than original Tammy, and just a tad more eye makeup. Her extra markings are "T-12-E" on her head and "T-12" on her back.

Finally, in the tradition of Mulligan Stew, Grown Up Pos'n Tammy was made. Both grown up and bendable, she has the same markings as Grown Up Tammy.

By 1964, Tammy was blessed with a family. Mom, Dad, sister Pepper and brothers Ted and Pete are not easily recognized by most collectors and are often passed over at flea markets and antique malls.

Tammy dolls were also manufactured in Canada by the Reliable Toy Company. The face and body molds were the same used for the American Tammys, but the markings were different. Canadian Tammys are marked "c Ideal Toy Corp/Reliable/Made in Canada/CANADA" on their backs.

Pos'N Pepper: Tammy's
little sister; NRFB.
*(Photo courtesy
of Linda Ladd.)*

A group of **Tammys** in their
well-made original outfits.
(Photo by the author.)

In September of 1964, Tammy dolls were marketed in Italy. They were the very first dolls to be advertised on television in Italy and the American-style commercials caused a storm of enthusiasm. Tammy knocked the Italian doll market on its ear, and eventually hundreds of thousands of the dolls were sold in Italy.

Many dolls sprang up imitating the Tammy look, including Penny Brite, Patty Duke and Mary Poppins. Remembering that imitation is the highest form of flattery helps us to realize what a striking individual she was in the world of dolls.

In 1962, Maria Fletcher was crowned Miss America; Jacqueline Kennedy was giving television audiences tours of the White House; the Twist was invented by a group of teenagers in New Jersey; and a wholesome-looking little doll, with doe eyes and roses in her cheeks, worked her way into the hearts of hundreds of thousands of people all over the world. She was Ideal's Tammy.

TAMMY RECORDS

Extremely hard to find are the record albums featuring great photography of Tammy in various outfits. Produced by Little World Records, the examples pictured here are:

#LW 902   "Tammy's Favorite Fairy Tales"
#LW 905   "Tammy in Fairyland"
#LW 901   "Meet Tammy and Her Friends"
#LW 904   "Tammy's Big Parade"
#LW 903   "Tammy's Sing-A-Long Party"

There is also said to be a Christmas Album! Even if the record itself is found in damaged condition, these album covers are worth saving and framing!

Tammy Record: **"Meet Tammy and Her Friends."** *(Photos courtesy of the J. Lawrence Collection.)*

Two Tammy Records: **"Tammy's Favorite Fairy Tales"** and **"Tammy in Fairyland."** *(Photos courtesy of the J. Lawrence Collection.)*

Two Tammy Record: **"Tammy's Big Parade"** and **"Tammy's Sing-A-Long Party."** *(Photos courtesy of the J. Lawrence Collection.)*

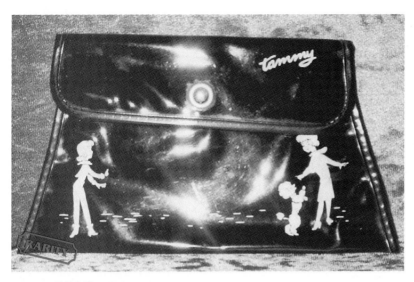

Tammy Child-Size Purse.
(Photo courtesy of Linda Ladd.)

Tammy Hair Dryer Case.
(Photo courtesy of Linda Ladd.)

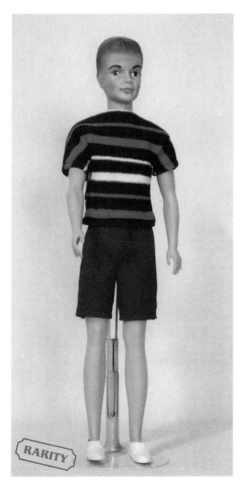

Bud.
*(Photos courtesy of the
J. Lawrence Collection.)*

TAMMY CHILD-SIZE PURSE

.This item is so rare that for years it was thought to be just a rumor! I know of the existence of only one. It is black patent leather, five-inches high by 8¹/₂-inches long, with a snap closure. The front features Tammy's name and two drawings of the doll. "Ideal" is not stamped anywhere on purse—so it could be a foreign knock-off!

TAMMY HAIR DRYER CASE

Here is another really rare item: the Tammy Hair Dryer Case. It came in both round and square versions, with a battery-operated doll-sized hair dryer inside that made a blowing noise. The square case measures 8¹/₄ × 8¹/₄ inches.

BUD

In 1965, Ideal produced a boyfriend for Tammy named Bud. Younger than Dad and more handsome than Ted, he resembles a kind of cross between two Georges—Maharis and Hamilton. He was 12¹/₂-inches tall, and is considered the rarest of Tammy family dolls.

PATTI

Because she was only sold through one store—Montgomery Ward—and for a short time period (Christmas 1964 and 1965), Patti is probably the second rarest Tammy family doll. She was promoted as Pepper's new playmate and sold originally for $1.74! A cute doll with hair that is, unfortunately, prone to frizziness, she is marked "c IDEAL TOY CORP/G 9 - L and G9-W2."

Patti is shown here wearing a variation of the Pepper outfit, **"Anchors away!"**
(Photo courtesy of Linda Ladd.)

Patti.
(Photo courtesy of the J. Lawrence Collection.)

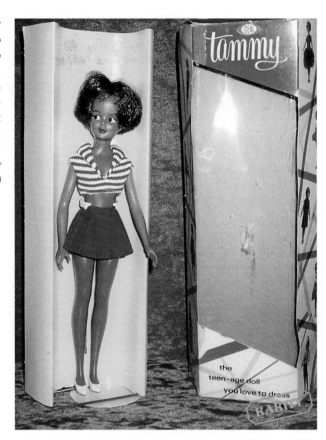

Black Tammy

Produced in 1965, the Black Tammy doll was a dark version of the Grown Up Tammy model, described earlier. Therefore, she is just slightly smaller than the standard Tammys, with a slimmer torso and shorter hair. She has the same markings as the Grown Up Tammy. The doll actually has beautiful coloring and is ardently sought after by today's Tammy collectors.

Carrot Top Pepper

Tammy's cute little sister was usually a blonde. An uncommon variation is an eye-popping redhead, known to collectors as "Carrot Top Pepper." She is 9¼-inches tall is like the standard Pepper in every other way except for her hair color.

Carrot Top Pepper.
(Photo courtesy of the J. Lawrence Collection.)

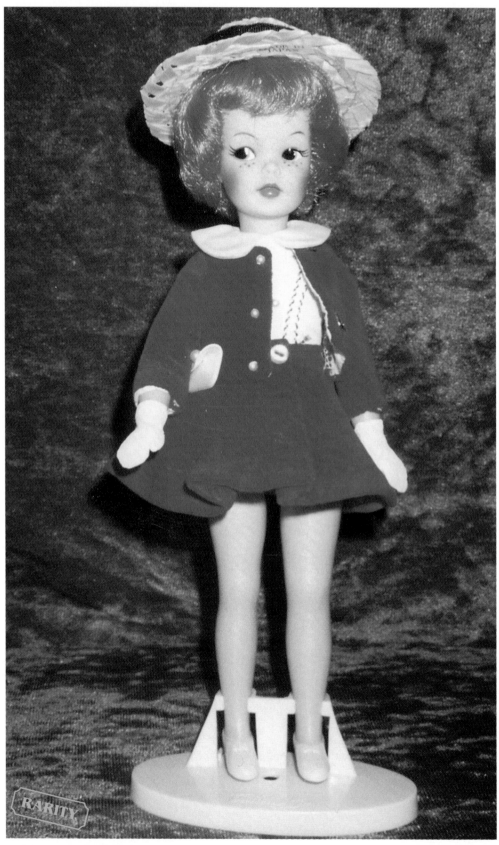

Another example of a **Carrot Top Pepper** which shows her beautiful coloring.
Here she is wearing **"Miss Gadabout,"** a hard-to-find Pepper outfit.
(Photo courtesy of Linda Ladd.)

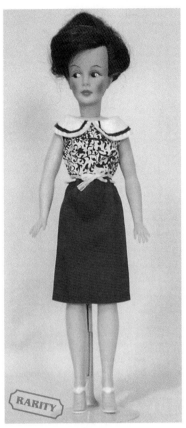

Brunette Mom.
*(Photo courtesy of the
J. Lawrence Collection.)*

Pete and Salty.
*(Photo courtesy of the
J. Lawrence Collection.)*

BRUNETTE MOM

Tammy's Mom was made as a platinum blonde. An unusual and hard-to-find variation is the Brunette Mom, standing 12$\frac{1}{2}$-inches tall and marked "IDEAL TOY CORP/W-13-L," and "W-13."

PETE AND SALTY

Pete (Tammy's little brother) and Salty (Pepper's little friend), were actually the same doll in different outfits. Pete had patched denim jeans, and Salty had red cotton play pants. Both had brown molded hair, freckles, and more than their share of cute. Marked "c 1964 IDEAL TOY CORP/P-8," both are really hard to find.

Tammy Lunchboxes.
(Photo courtesy of the J. Lawrence Collection.)

BRUNETTE STRAIGHT-LEG TAMMY

Considered hard to find, and rising in popularity, is the brunette straight-leg Tammy. The example on the left, in green, is wearing "Private Secretary,"—a hard-to-find outfit!

TAMMY LUNCHBOXES

These lunchbox and thermos sets featuring artwork of Tammy and Pepper were made by Aladdin and are favorites among collectors. They are very hard to find.

Brunette Straight-Leg Tammy.
(Photo courtesy of the J. Lawrence Collection.)

**Tammy and
Ted Catamaran.**
*(Photo courtesy
of Linda Ladd.)*

RARITY

Tammy Thermos.
(Photo courtesy of Linda Ladd.)

TAMMY AND
TED CATAMARAN

This well-made play boat puts many of today's toys to shame. Stock #9706-5, it was made in 1964 and is eighteen-inches long by twenty-three-inches high, and really floats. Very hard to find, especially in the box, it is a sought-after collectible. Even the paper dolls that came with the set are desirable!

TAMMY LUNCHBOX THERMOS

The Tammy lunchbox sets, made by Aladdin, are real finds for the collector. The thermos alone is enough to make any collector's day. This is the type of item that can still be picked up for a song at a flea market, for a fraction of what it would be worth to a collector.

TAMMY'S JUKE BOX

This wonderfully detailed piece shows a rack of tiny records, and a listing of selections under different categories of music, such as popular, classical and jazz. There is a wind-up mechanism that plays "Music, Music, Music." There are rumors of these juke boxes playing other tunes. This item is also a collectible to anyone who enjoys '50s and '60s paraphernalia.

Tammy's Juke Box.
(Photo courtesy of Linda Ladd.)

Box and contents of **Tammy's Bed/ Dresser/Chair** set. *(Photos courtesy of Linda Ladd.)*

RARITY

TAMMY'S BED/ DRESSER/CHAIR SET

Tammy's Bed/Dresser/Chair set is hard to find, especially in its original box. This set could be purchased in 1964 through the Sears, Wards, and Spiegel Christmas Catalogs.

Tammy Pencil Case—another potential flea market find, marked "1963 Ideal." *(Photo courtesy of Linda Ladd.)*

Tammy's bright blue convertible with the white wall tires, in its original box! *(Photo courtesy of Linda Ladd.)*

HARD-TO-FIND TAMMY CASES

Tammy had a variety of storage cases for dolls and clothes. The Model Miss Case, shown here, is an oversized case that is very hard to find. The interior is lined in white vinyl with the "Tammy" name, and the trunk has a tremendous amount of storage space along with a small mirror.

Exterior of **Model Miss Case.**
(Photo courtesy of Linda Ladd.)

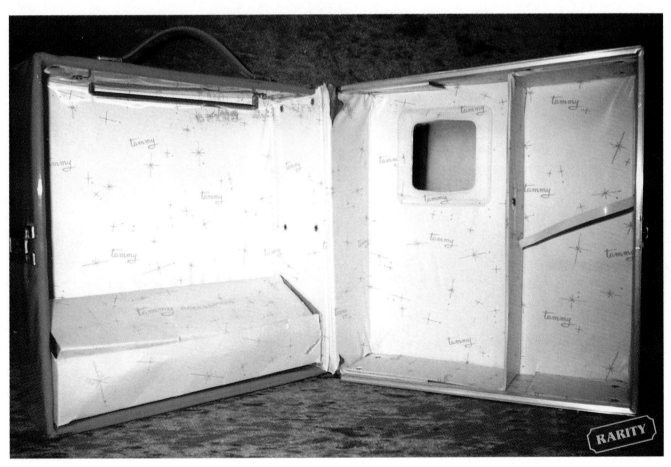

Interior of **Model Miss Case.**
(Photo courtesy of Linda Ladd.)

MISTY/TAMMY TELEPHONE BOOTH CASE

In 1965, Ideal introduced another Tammy-sized doll named Glamour Misty. Many outfits and accessories from that time on were marked or tagged "TAMMY/MISTY" or "MISTY/TAMMY." The Misty/Tammy Telephone Booth Case depicted here has so far been extremely hard to find. A most unique case in its design, it is also unusual in that it shows Misty on its cover as a brunette.

Misty/Tammy Telephone Booth Case.
(Photo courtesy of Linda Ladd.)

TAMMY/MISTY OUTFITS

The outfits tagged "Tammy/Misty" were the last outfits made for Tammy and are harder to find than her other outfits. It is believed that the very last of these outfits came on a card with no cardboard frame, as original warehouse stock has been found that way. These Tammy/Misty outfits present a fun challenge to the collector who thought s/he had everything. Shown here is #9959-8, Winter Weather.

Here are examples of some of the earlier Tammy/Misty outfits that came in a cardboard frame.

#9959-8, Winter Weather.
(Photo courtesy of Linda Ladd.)

This breath-taking brunette shows the allure of a mint Tammy doll. As you can see, her face painting is first-rate and her actual coloring is strikingly beautiful, like a China doll. The original sheen on an early Tammy's hair is always wonderful. She is wearing **"Fraternity Hop."** This great '60s outfit, especially its stole, is very hard to find.
(Photo courtesy of Linda Ladd.)

(L-R) **"Beau and Arrow"**; **"Dance Date."**
(Photos courtesy of Linda Ladd.)

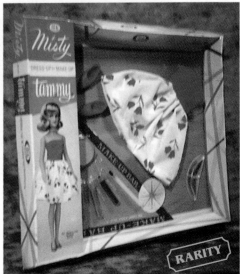

The fur stole and garland of **"Fur and Formal"** are very hard-to-find items. *(Photo courtesy of Linda Ladd.)*

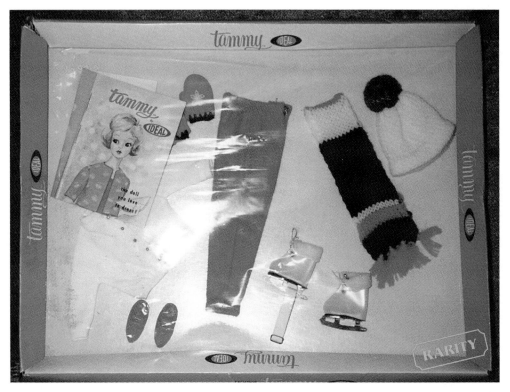

The skates on Tammy's **"Figure 8"** outfit (#9212) are particularly hard to find, as are the mittens. *(Photo courtesy of Linda Ladd.)*

Two **Sasha Ginghams.**

106

SASHA RARITIES

*I*n 1964, *Life* magazine spotlighted the handmade dolls of Sasha Morgenthaler in a spread which included an article and photos. Very few dolls have been featured in major, "non-doll" magazines, and the Sasha dolls were no doubt selected because of their unique design and distinctive look.

Their designer, Sasha Morgenthaler, was born in 1893, and became in life, a gifted sculptor, painter and mother. Like Käthe Kruse, she began making dolls for her own children in the 1920s and ended up creating dolls of such eye-catching charm that her labor of love became a full time, very successful business. She passed away in 1975, but her dolls continued to be produced for eleven years after her death.

Sasha dolls have a slim, tapered gracefulness about them. Their limbs are pleasingly long and thin and are ball jointed for versatile posing. Their angular faces have a gentle, quiet beauty that is, so far, matchless in the doll world. One may come across Shirley Temple look-alikes, Ginny and Barbie look-alikes, etc.; but in my own experience, there has never been a Sasha look-alike. All of the dolls, even the platinum blondes, have dark, cafe-au-lait colored skin, which is their most striking feature. This color skin is never seen on dolls fashioned as Caucasians and is the very hallmark of Sasha dolls. The painted features are subtle, with a hazy watercolor quality; and their construction is of heavy, seemingly solid vinyl. Sashas are outfitted in simple, but very well-made clothing, meant to endure the rigors of play.

At the time of the *Life* magazine article, Mrs. Morgenthaler was only producing about 150 dolls a year. Acting as both designer and crafter, she sold her dolls for between $50 and $150 each, certainly not a trivial price for 1964. Their singularity and appeal easily commanded the substantial price tag, but on her own she could produce only a limited number each year. Following the published article, the molds were sold to a company in England which began to mass produce the dolls from 1969-1986.

I can remember the hubbub at area doll shows and doll club meetings, when it was announced in 1986 that Sasha dolls were no longer going to be produced. Dealers and collectors alike were buying up as many as they could afford, speculating that the dolls' prices would skyrocket. And, as predicted, they did. Special Edition Sashas which sold in the early 1980s for around $150 can now command anywhere from $300-450 today if mint in box. Please note that these prices refer to the special limited editions, and not to the largely produced Sashas, such as "Gingham."

The author's daughter
Tiffin, at four, with one
of her "twins."
(Photo by the author.)

The three basic types of Sasha dolls are the sixteen-inch girl
(Sasha), the sixteen-inch boy (Gregor), and the twelve-inch baby
(Sasha Baby). All have the same body construction and painted features. The mass produced versions of these dolls, originally priced at
about $50, currently sell for about $200, if mint in box. The dolls are
unmarked, but came originally with a wrist tag showing the red, white
and blue circular Sasha logo.

My daughter received two blonde Sasha Ginghams from my mother for her fourth birthday—her "twins," because the dolls resembled

her so much. After an estimated 500 tea parties and about 10,000 hours logged in the sandbox, they look as pristine as the day she tore the wrapping off of them. As play dolls they are tenacious and durable. Their bodies are solid and sturdy and there are no sleep eyes to cloud up or jam. Children love them. As investments, they have thus far proven to be sound. And finally, as a cherished find by the collector, they are truly objects of beauty; unique and with a style all their own—the culmination of one woman's concept and exacting standards of quality.

Although the following Sasha dolls are not rarities in terms of numbers alone, and in the same sense of the word as the other dolls in this book, they are being featured for specific reasons. They are limited issues with productions ranging from 4,000 to 6,000, much larger numbers than, for instance, the Effanbee limited editions. But Sasha owners are far less likely to part with them, making the market much tighter. Many collectors have never had the opportunity to even see these dolls, which is why I decided to include them.

Velvet.
(Photo courtesy of Sally Broome.)

VELVET

Only 5,000 of these simple but elegant dolls were issued in 1981.

PINTUCKS

A true beauty is this 1982 limited edition—"Pintucks"—so named for the bit of heirloom sewing technique used on her white cotton dress. Some 6,000 of these dolls were produced.

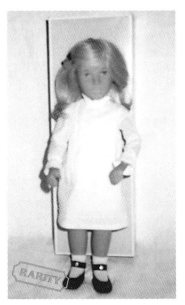

Pintucks.
(Photo courtesy of Sally Broome.)

KILTIE

A stunning redhead in a classically-styled dress is Kiltie, issued in 1983 and limited to a production of 4,000.

HARLEQUIN

A less formally attired Sasha with her sandals and guitar is this Harlequin, issued in 1984 and limited to a production of 4,000.

Kiltie.
(Photo courtesy of Sally Broome.)

  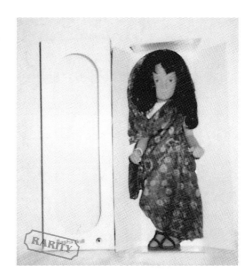

L-R: **Harlequin;**
Prince Gregor; Sari.
*(Photos courtesy
of Sally Broome.)*

PRINCE GREGOR

A little boy was produced in 1985, and limited to a production of 4,000.

PRINCESS

Princess was issued in 1986, just short of the company closing its doors.

SARI

Although she was not a limited issue, Sari was produced in 1986, the last year of the company's existence. For that reason, her production was cut short, making her harder to find.

ALEXANDERKIN RARITIES

Few faces in all of the realm of modern dolls have been as precious and heart-melting as the faces of Madame Alexander's Alexanderkins. They stand head and shoulders above all other miniature (seven to eight inch) dolls, not only because of their exclusive beauty, but also because of their history. From 1953 to the present day, the Madame Alexander Doll Company has manufactured the most engaging dolls, with the most extensive and exquisite wardrobes, under the categories of Internationals, Wendy Anns, Maggie Mix-Ups, Storybooks, and Little Women—all known collectively to doll lovers as "Alexanderkins."

Ginnys, Pams, Gingers, etc. have come close, and can proudly stand next to these little charmers on a display shelf. But no doll of this kind can actually equal their eloquence, for their mere presence speaks volumes about the quality, standards and workmanship of a bygone era, and reveals a unique vision that was Madame Alexander's alone.

Always aware of the special bond between children and dolls, Madame's instinctive understanding of how very precious these dolls are shows through in their design. The wardrobes for these lucky little eight-inchers include miniature laces, tiny buttons, pintucks, ribbon beading, embroidery, rhinestones, pearls, felt flowers, braided trims, heirloom bonnets, dotted Swiss, organdy, tulle and taffeta. Party dresses and pinafores, feathers and flounces, tutus and tiny tiaras—they are the essence of what doll-dreams are made of. There are not enough words to truly do justice to the charm and beauty of these special little dolls. Pat Smith's 1985 book, however, *The World of Alexanderkins*, with its scores of pictures, can help.

Issued as straight-leg non-walkers, straight-leg walkers, and bend-knee walkers and non-walkers, these dolls are constructed of hard plastic with glued-on wigs. Once you familiarize yourself with these little dolls, they are easy to identify.

Of the Alexanderkins from the 1950s, the following are considered hard to find: (BKW= bend-knee walker; SLW= straight-leg walker/ SLNW= straight-leg non-walker).

◆ Aunt Pitty Pat (1957-BKW)

◆ Baby Angel (1955-SLW)

◆ Baby Clown (1955-SLW)

- ✦ Cousin Karen (1956-BKW)
- ✦ Guardian Angel (1954-SLNW)
- ✦ Maggie Mixup Pink Angel (1960-BKW)
- ✦ Maggie Mixup Angel (1961-BKW, either blue or white)
- ✦ Parlour Maid (1956-BKW)
- ✦ Peter Pan (1953-SLNW)
- ✦ Pierrot Clown (1956-BKW)

And within that same time frame, the following Alexanderkins are considered very rare:

- ✦ Queen Esther (1954-SLNW)
- ✦ Miriam (1954-SLNW)
- ✦ Nana Governess (1957-BKW)
- ✦ Ruth (1954-SLNW)
- ✦ Rachael (1954-SLNW)
- ✦ Jacob (1954-SLNW)
- ✦ Joseph (1954-SLNW)
- ✦ Samuel (1954-SLNW)
- ✦ Juliet (1955-SLW)
- ✦ Lady in Waiting (1955-SLW)
- ✦ Rodeo (1955-SLW)
- ✦ Romeo (1955-SLW)

And the following Alexanderkins are considered extremely rare:

Infant of Prague (1957-BK): These dolls were specially made for a religious goods company, I. Donnelly, and were then dressed by the Sisters of Mercy, a Catholic order of nuns dedicated to, among other things, the religious education of young children. It seems as though only the doll itself and the outer skeleton of the crown was supplied by the Alexander Doll Company, and that all of the fabric, trim and beading was supplied by this group of Sisters in Omaha, Nebraska. The doll's right hand was specifically molded to resemble the gesture seen in religious paintings of the Infant of Prague.

Little Minister (1957-BKW): This doll had a side-part boy's haircut, in a reddish brown. He wore a black minister's gown, a white lace-trimmed overvestment, and a brocade stole. Also included were a small Bible, a crucifix on a chain, and a pair of tortoise shell-colored eyeglasses.

Wendy Ann Dresser Set (1953-SLNW): This brunette Wendy Ann in her bright yellow pinafore came with an entire cardboard dresser filled with tiny accessories and extra outfits. For obvious reasons, it is very hard to find this set completely intact.

MADAME ALEXANDER'S PATTY

Another very hard-to-find Madame Alexander doll is eighteen-inch Patty, made for one year only—1965. She has the Caroline face and is a vinyl toddler-style doll.

Madame Alexander's Patty.
(Photo courtesy of Grace Frowd.)

OTHER ALEXANDER HARD-TO-FINDS OR RARITIES

The Cynthia doll, made by Madame Alexander in 1953, is also considered a rare doll by collectors. She is a Black, hard plastic, little girl doll with slim and graceful lines. A very dark-skinned beauty with sleep eyes and a glued-on wig, she came in fourteen-, eighteen- and twenty-two-inch sizes, and is marked "ALEX" on her head.

Sister Belle.
(Photo by the author.)

MATTEL RARITIES

Started out of a garage in 1945, the Mattel Toy Company hit it big in 1960—a year after the introduction of the Barbie doll—and moved its headquarters to Hawthorne, California. Another big seller for this company was introduced in 1960: The Chatty Cathy doll. The public's response to Chatty Cathy and Barbie, as well as another line to follow, called Liddle Kiddles, helped to make Mattel the toy giant that it is today. These three dolls are discussed individually in earlier chapters, as their celebrity warrants it, but there has been a notable parade of other well-made and inventive dolls by Mattel that merit attention: Sister Belle, Mattie Mattel, Shrinking Violet, Casper the Ghost, Drowsy and Scooba Doo (1961-1964)—all cloth dolls with talking mechanisms. All were fairly popular in their day, with their soft, huggable charm and engaging facial expressions.

Baby's Hungry, Baby First Step, Baby See & Say, Dancerina (1966-1971): Some of the hard plastic and vinyl mechanical dolls were, with some exceptions relating to their mechanical workings, generally well-made structurally. All of these dolls had winning faces and could do a variety of things such as walk, chew, suck on a bottle, roll eyes, read nursery rhymes, pedal a tricycle, or dance.

Baby Secret (left) and **Hi Dottie** (right), two Mattel Talkers in the condition in which they are most often found.
(Photo by the author.)

115

**Small Talks and
Small Walks** by Mattel.
(Photo by the author.)

Small Talks and Small Walks (1968-1970): An absolutely darling group of scaled-down walkers and talkers, whose walking mechanisms and voice boxes seem to have survived the years well. The faces on these dolls reach a pinnacle of cuteness, with all of them bearing a recognizable "family resemblance." This line included Baby Small Talk, Baby Small Walk, Swingy, and the Storybooks such as Cinderella, Goldilocks and Little Bo Peep.

Cheerful Tearful (1965-1966): With a very well received gimmick behind her, this doll, whose face could change from a grin to a grimace with a wave of her arm, almost reached "household word" status.

Baby Tenderlove (1969-on): This very popular baby, conceived in 1969, started a succession of future Tenderloves too numerous to mention (Talking Baby Tenderlove, Living Baby Tenderlove, etc.) She seems to mark the start of an era when Mattel's standards of design and aesthetics began to loosen up considerably. It seems that a large majority of the dolls from this time period onward all had the same platinum blonde hair, nondescript painted eyes rather than sleep eyes, and many have even used a cheaper vinyl that almost pitted with age.

Tiny Cheerful Tearful.

Cynthia (1971): This exceptionally attractive doll may well have been inspired by the success of the Brady Bunch TV series. Standing nineteen-inches tall, she looks like Marcia, sounds like Marcia and has Cindy's name (sorry Jan, I guess it's "Marcia, Marcia, Marcia!" again). She was a mannequin-style talker which used small plastic records that were inserted into her side. The records allowed her to say a few phrases at a time, rather than one short phrase, as with the pull-string talkers. Her face and form were absolutely beautiful, and both her and Tomy's Kimberly have, arguably, the best hair in modern dolling. Silky and brilliant, it is a shame that Mattel hasn't used this "recipe" for hair more often!

Cynthia.

MATTEL RARITIES

Some of the following Mattel Rarities uncovered:

Black Baby Small Talk: Most of the dolls in this absolutely darling line were white. The Black Baby Small Talk is very hard to find.

Honey Blonde Buffy: This doll, also considered a small talk, was patterned after the character of Buffy from the TV series "Family Affair," starring Brian Keith and Sebastian Cabot. The actress who played Buffy, Anissa Jones, died at a young age. Many Baby Boomers remember her fondly, which makes this a popular and sought after doll. Most of the Buffy dolls made had a reddish hair color. Harder to find is the honey blonde variation.

Casper, Matty Mattel, and Sister Belle with Holes in Eyes and Mouth: The first soft-body talkers had holes in the back of their heads for their "voice" sounds. The later issues, which are harder to come by, have holes in the dolls' eyes and mouth for this same purpose.

GREEN-EYED SINGIN' CHATTY

This tail-ender to the Chatty family was produced in 1964 and came as either a blonde or a brunette with blue eyes. She had an impish face that was peppered with freckles. Only two "sightings" of a green-eyed version have materialized that I know of, making her a real enigma. Mattel in the 1960s had a tendency to be a very frugal company that used up all their remaining resources at the end of a production sequence, in a waste not/want not effort to economize. Happily, this has made for many interesting variations among their mass-produced dolls. Singing' Chatty was a seventeen-inch mannequin-style pull-string talker who sang nursery rhymes.

The **Brunette Singin' Chatty,** left, has green eyes. *(Dolls courtesy of Terry Carter. Photo by Patti Cooke.)*

STORYBOOK SMALL TALKS

Mattel's Storybook Small Talks are play dolls from the '60s that are now considered collectible. Dolls that were considered collectible 30 years ago are often found in good shape and with original clothing because they were kept that way. When collectors take a shine to dolls that were considered play dolls 30 years ago, however, it is quite a different story. Original outfits and original hairsets are hard to come by, as, of course, they were played with. Pictured here are some Storybook Small Talks in their original outfits, now considered hard to find.

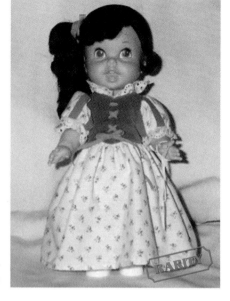

Snow White.
(Photo courtesy of Steven Carissimo.)

All of these Small Talks are from about 1969-1970. **Bo Peep** (far left); **Goldilocks** (lower right); and **Cinderella** (upper right). Cinderella has a paler complexion than other Storybooks and she has violet eyes.
(Photos courtesy of Steven Carissimo.)

Valerie. *(Photo courtesy of Steven Carissimo.)*

VALERIE

Here is a rather obscure little doll with quite a bit of crossover appeal. She is Mattel's Valerie with Growin' Pretty Hair, probably made in response to the enormous popularity of the Crissy Family of Grow Hair dolls by Ideal. She appeals to Small Talk collectors because she used the same head mold; she appeals to collectors of grow-hair dolls; and she appeals to anyone looking for something unusual. An extremely cute doll, she is very hard to find, especially MIB, and many collectors do not even know of her existence.

Baby Teenietalk.
(Photo courtesy of Steven Carissimo.)

BABY TEENIETALK

Here is another unusual Mattel doll whose face resembles both Dee Dee and Baby Secrets. She is Baby Teenietalk, a little known Mattel talker that may be of interest to collectors of Mattel talking dolls. Her rarity is hard to determine, but apparently most collectors of Mattel talkers have not even heard of her. Made around 1967, she is pictured here in what is believed to be her original outfit.

Cathy Quickcurl.
(Photo courtesy of Steven Carissimo.)

CATHY QUICKCURL

Another unusual Mattel doll with a Small Talk/Hi Dottie-type face, Quickcurl Barbie-type hair, and a Chatty Cathy-type name. I have been unable to find this doll in a doll reference book, and know of only two collectors who have heard of her. This is believed to be her original outfit, and she came with a curling wand, brush, curlers and an instruction booklet. Her hair has fine copper wires that allow it to be easily curled. This doll was made around 1974.

TROLL RARITIES

"*D*eep in the forests of Scandinavia, where the dark pines loom and pale lichens spot the rocks, there dwell a strange and little-known folk. No one knows how long they have been there, nor how they first came into the world. But it is clear that they are an ancient race—so ancient, in fact, that the pines, the lichens, even the rocks feel young when they pass by . . . . They are the trolls."

—from the **Troll Book,**
by Michael Cerenstein
(Random House, 1980)

American made Trolls, (left, right and foreground) and **Denmark Trolls.** Notice the darker vinyl used for the Denmark-made versions. *(Photo courtesy of Lynn Schelitzche.)*

A gathering of Trolls by **Dam, Uneeda, S.H.E.** and spin-off companies. Values: $15 in outfits, about $25 for the Black Troll, and $30 for the two-headed mermaid.
(Photo courtesy of Lynn Schelitzche.)

Some of the great dolls in history—Raggedy Anns, Käthe Kruse dolls, Sashas, and more—have had their beginnings in the simple act of a parent crafting a doll for their child as a gift from the heart. It was during the 1950s that Thomas Dam, a baker in Denmark, carved little troll dolls for his children out of wood. As with all good things, word got around. Friends told friends, who told other friends, and before long a factory was built to keep up with the demand for these lovably homely little creatures, now produced in vinyl.

As word spread to the United States, a factory in Florida was assigned to produce the Dam brand of Trolls for the American market. Wanting to cash in on a gold mine, other American toy companies started to produce their own lines of Trolls, including Uneeda (Wishniks Trolls) and Scandia House Enterprises (S.H.E. Trolls).

The Trolls that were originally manufactured by Dam in Denmark are of a darker and softer vinyl than those produced in the United States, which are of the more familiar, lighter, and more rigid vinyl.

The original Dam brand of Trolls were marked on the doll's back or foot, but later issues were marked with stickers that could be peeled off.

The invasion of Trolls in the 1960s made an impression on all of us. Even if you didn't own one, you certainly can remember seeing one, as their matchless little mugs are hard to forget.

Quite a variety of Troll outfits were created and by a variety of companies. **Outfits for three-inch Trolls,** MIP, are valued at about $15; for **six-inch Trolls,** MIP, about $25; and for **eight-inch Trolls,** about $40.
(Photo courtesy of Lynn Schelitzche.)

DENMARK TROLLS

The trolls manufactured by Dam in Denmark are much harder to find than the bounty of American-made Trolls. The early Trolls are marked, but the really distinguishing feature of these Danish Trolls is the darker, softer vinyl used in their construction. These Trolls from Denmark are the most pricey among collectors.

Animal Trolls produced by Dam in Denmark are more rare than the regular Trolls. This three-inch Denmark reindeer is valued at about $100. The turtle is especially rare and is valued at about $200.

L-R: Denmark **Reindeer** and **Turtle.** *(Photos courtesy of Lynn Schelitzche.)*

Large monkeys made in Denmark are valued at about $200-300; small monkeys are valued at about $140. *(Photo courtesy of Lynn Schelitzche.)*

The 6-inch **Palace Guard,** made in Denmark, is valued at about $175. *(Photo courtesy of Lynn Schelitzche.)*

The lion at left is made of Denmark vinyl and is valued at about $130. The lion at right is of American vinyl and is valued at about $60. Lions are the most common among the larger Troll animals, but are still considered hard to find.
(Photo courtesy of Lynn Schelitzche.)

The Giraffe made in Denmark (left) is valued at about $175; the American-made giraffe (right) is valued at about $80.
(Photo courtesy of Lynn Schelitzche.)

The cows on the left are of Denmark vinyl. The large version, with collar and bell, is valued at about $250; the small version is valued at about $60. The cows on the right are of American vinyl. The large version, with collar and bell, is valued at about $130; the small version shown in its box is valued at about $55. The clothed small version is valued at about $45, and the nude small version is valued at about $30.
(Photo courtesy of Lynn Schelitzche.)

The gray elephant, left, was made in Denmark and is valued at about $250, with his collar and bell. The two elephants on the right are American made, and are valued at about $175 for the large version and $35 for the small version.
(Photo courtesy of Lynn Schelitzche.)

ENGLISH TROLLS

The Dam brand of Trolls also had a factory in England. The Viking boy on the left was made in Denmark, but the Viking girl, right, was produced in England. English Trolls are of rigid vinyl, similar to American-made Trolls, but are a bit orange in color with pronounced cheek blush. Each is valued at about $100.

Viking Boy and **Viking Girl.**
(Photo courtesy of Lynn Schelitzche.)

Brides, Grooms and Santas are hard to find and sought after by collectors. Pictured in the back row, center, are the twelve-inch (a rare size also) Dam Bride and Groom, valued at about $175 each. The six-inch couples (center row) by Wishnik, Dam and S.H.E. range in value from $15-$30. Grooms are harder to find in the six-inch size. *(Photo courtesy of Lynn Schelitzche.)*

Back row: six-inch Dam ($45); eight-inch Dam ($50); eight-inch Dam with mustache ($90); twelve-inch Dam ($200); eight-inch with rooted hair ($50); six-inch Scandia House ($40). **Middle row:** three-inch Santas ($25); ornament in center ($40). **Front row:** Pencil toppers and Merry Christmas Troll ($15-$20). The most common Santa Troll is an eight-inch Dam without mustache. *(Photo courtesy of Lynn Schelitzche.)*

This is a very special little guy. Dam created a specific face mold just for him which melts the hearts of Troll people and non-Troll people alike. The emotions conveyed by his eyes, facial expression and pose make him a work of art. At five-inches tall, he has molded clothes and shoes, another unique feature. Considered rare, he is valued at about $200. *(Photo courtesy of Lynn Schelitzche.)*

Superhero Trolls.
(Photo courtesy of Lynn Schelitzche.)

SUPERHERO TROLLS

Superhero Trolls are also hard to find and have a crossover appeal to those who collect superheroes. The Bat Cave cases pictured in the back row were sold through the Montgomery Ward Christmas catalog. The 1965 Bat Cave (with the car) is valued at about $150, and the 1966 Bat Cave (with the car) is valued at about $150. The 1966 Bat Cave (without car) is valued at about $100. The six-inch Superheroes in the center row and their approximate values are, left to right, Wishnik Batman with regular or bug-out eyes ($40), Superman ($60), Green Hornet ($90), Dam Captain Lightning, shown without his mask, ($70), Scandia House Batman and Scandia House Wasp ($60). All three-inch Superheroes in the front row are valued at about $25.

Six-inch Black Bride.
*(Photo courtesy of
Lynn Schelitzche.)*

BLACK TROLLS

Black Trolls are considered rare, as are Trolls with eyelashes. Brides are a special find. This six-inch Black Bride with eyelashes is almost too good to be true. Made by Dam, she is valued at about $150. Other rare variations are red, orange or green Trolls; Trolls with earrings or tails; and Trolls with two-toned hair.

Seated Pixie Trolls.
(Photo courtesy of Lynn Schelitzche.)

Three-inch Trollette.
*(Photo courtesy of
Lynn Schelitzche.)*

Pixie Trolls

The Seated Pixie Trolls are considered rare. Their pose makes them extra cute, another desirable trait for collectibles. Made by Royalty Designs of Florida, they are valued at between $30 and $35, depending on outfit.

Three-inch Trollettes

The Three-inch Trollettes, manufactured by Dam, are considered very difficult to find. They came in a variety of formal wear and were packaged in clear plastic domes. When in original packaging, values fall between $50 and $100, depending on outfit and the personal preference of the collector.

Packaged Trolls

Most Trolls were not sold in any kind of packaging, so to find one in its original box or bag is especially rare. The Wishnik Family in its original box (center) is valued at about $150. The six-inch Wishniks in cylinder, about $45; the eight-inch version in bag, about $90; three-inch Wishnik in bag, $20; three-inch Wishnik in cylinder, $15 nude, $20 clothed.

Packaged Washnik Trolls.
(Photo courtesy of Lynn Schelitzche.)

More Trolls in their original packaging. From left to right, with their approximate values, they are three-inch Dam in bag ($20); two three-inch Dams in plastic boxes, ($25); six-inch Dam in bag, made of the darker, softer Denmark vinyl, ($60); S.H.E. Astronaut pencil topper, ($25); and three three-inch S.H.E. Trolls in cylinders ($25).
(Photo courtesy of Lynn Schelitzche.)

Here are two examples of some unique original packaging. The Bunallen Company made a limited number of these 3-D scenes for Trolls made by both Dam and S.H.E. Considered very rare, they are valued at between $50 and $75, depending on individual preference.
(Photo courtesy of Lynn Schelitzche.)

Various **Ceramic Troll** dolls. *(Photo courtesy of Lynn Schelitzche.)*

CERAMIC TROLLS

Also hard to find are Ceramic Troll dolls, so uncommon that many collectors have never even heard of them. In the back row are three four-inch "nodders" with inscriptions on their base. Made in Japan, they are valued at about $35 boxed, and about $20 without a box. Next is the eight-inch Neanderthal Man made by Bijou, which is extremely rare. He is valued at about $90. The eighteen-inch bank in the center, by Sylvestri, is valued at about $110. The Lucky Bank boy or girl, made in Japan, is valued at about $35, and the three sports "nodders" to the right are valued at about $60. The ceramic Trolls in the front row are all made in Denmark by Dam, and are valued at about $75 each.

TROLL HOUSES

These Troll Houses are great collectibles and have a charm all their own, even if you're not a fan of the Troll dolls. Most of the basic and more common Troll houses are valued at about $25. Pictured are two of the more rare houses—Troll House (front) and Troll Manor (back, with yellow roof). Each is valued at about $40. The Wishnik Log Car (center) is valued at about $50 with bumper sticker. The Troll Village, by Marx, (right) is valued at about $200, and the Marx Miniature Play Set, (right, front) is valued at about $100.

Various **Troll Houses.**
*(Photo courtesy
of Lynn Schelitzche.)*

OTHER RARE TROLL ITEMS

Again, **Hard-to-find paper products!** Troll coloring books are valued at about
$27; three-ring binder about $20; paper doll books, about $20; record
albums, about $35; joke book, about $15; patterns, about $10; and pencil
case, about $10. *(Photo courtesy of Lynn Schelitzche.)*

This **Thomas Dam Troll Book,** made in Denmark and written in Danish, is valued at about $35. *(Photo courtesy of Lynn Schelitzche.)*

Merchandise shaped in the image of a Troll presents a fun challenge for collectors to try to find. This **chocolate syrup bottle** is extremely rare, but opinions as to its value range from! $20-$200! *(Photo courtesy of Lynn Schelitzche.)*

Metal sculpture featuring Trolls, made by Sexton—a very rare piece. Valued at about $140. *(Photo courtesy of Lynn Schelitzche.)*

All rare items: **Troll cookie cutter,** valued at about $20; **whisky bottle,** valued at about $100; **salt and pepper shakers,** about $140.
(Photo courtesy of Lynn Schelitzche.)

These **Troll handle bar grips** were a Sears exclusive. They are valued at about $100, MIP, and about $25 each, loose.
(Photo courtesy of Lynn Schelitzche.)

The **Troll purse,** made by Bunallen, is valued at about $50.
(Photo courtesy of Lynn Schelitzche.)

The twelve-inch Trolls, made by Dam, are harder to find than other sizes. Shown here are twelve-inch Dams in rarer outfits—two **Farmer Boys, Farmer Girl, Caveman, Play Outfit, Eskimo,** and **Clown.** Trolls of this size in rarer outfits are valued at about $125.
(Photo courtesy of Lynn Schelitzche.)

Here is a group of eight-inch Dams in rarer outfits. From left to right in the back row are **Pirate Boy and Girl,** and **Raincoat Boy and Girl.** In the front row, left to right, are **Sailor, Artist, Robin Hood, Farmer Boy,** and **Scandinavian Girl.** Each is valued at about $40.
(Photo courtesy of Lynn Schelitzche.)

DAWN RARITIES

In 1970, a true novelty was born in the world of dolls. Dawn, a mere slip of a girl, hit the market and grabbed the attention of many. A miniaturized version of Barbie-types, she stood a slight 6½-inches, with dainty proportions and an exquisitely beautiful face. Her very delicate features were accented by thick flirty lashes and a brilliant mane of hair—quite an extraordinary amount of detail in one so small. The sheer originality of having a small-scale version of the popular eleven- to twelve-inch fashion dolls was a marketing masterpiece.

In her first year, 1970, Dawn was touted as the most successful doll ever, with 40 outfits and a variety of playsets. The original Dawn was very poseable—an advertised 100 possible positions in all. Dawn, a breathtaking blonde, had friends: Dale, a Black female with short curly hair; Angie, another beauty with waist-length brunette hair; and Glory, a radiant redhead with green eyes, straight hair and bangs.

Still dating after all these years, **Dawn** and **Gary** meet at **Dixie's Diner.**
(Photo by the author.)

A **Dawn** (left)
with two **Angies** (right).
(Photo by the author.)

In 1971, five new dolls, 75 additional outfits, and three new playsets were featured in a four million dollar television campaign—more than any manufacturer had ever spent on a single toy category in a single year. Her new associates were Jessica, with a short pageboy; Long Locks, with beautiful brown hair long enough to sit on; Gary, a dark-haired male; Ron, a light-haired male; and Van, a Black male. That same year, Dawn family dolls came as either regular or "dancing" versions. The dancing models had moving heads, hips, and legs that were activated by pumping an arm.

Dawn's playsets were innovative, imaginative and glamorous. Her Talking Sofa Telephone was a remarkable creation for the day. Entire two-way conversations between Dawn and her friends could be heard emanating from the French-styled telephone table, sofa and phone. Dawn's Beauty Pageant consisted of a stage and runway. Dawn's Disco was a dance floor with levers and knobs that activated Kevin and Fancy Feet—two Dawn dolls that were made to accompany the set. Dawn's Glamour Boutique had a full-length, gold-gilded, three-way mirror for Dawn to admire herself in. Dawn's Flower Fantasy Stands offered a sensational way for little girls to display their Dawn dolls. Five different varieties could hold one, two, or three dolls and were festooned with flowers. The Dawn Fashion Show had both a front and back revolving stage with the mechanics to cause Dawn to walk and turn by herself. Dawn Head to Toe dolls came with removable wigs and hair pieces. Also available was the Dawn Music Box, Beauty Parlor, a pink convertible, a remote control blue convertible, a red plastic Window Pocketbook, and both three- and six-doll carrying cases.

**Dawn's
Beauty Pageant.**
*(Photo courtesy of
Katerine Burrows.)*

Dawn Lunchbox sets.
(Photo courtesy of Christine Gunderson.)

Following is a list of what are believed to be the rarest Dawn dolls or items:

Gas Station Promotions: During Dawn's reign of popularity, certain gas stations offered a Dawn Doll ("Dad! Stop here!! Get some gas!! Quick!!") for a mere 99 cents with a fill up. Collectors have seen large posters, about six feet in height, promoting this marketing scheme, but I have yet to locate someone who owns one. Just what Dawn doll was given away with this promotion is unknown at this time. This poster is probably the rarest of all Dawn related items.

Green-Eyed Dale: Dale was a Black female doll in the Dawn family. She usually had either black or amber eyes, but rare exceptions were made with green eyes.

Lunchboxes: These vinyl lunchboxes, made by Alladin, are very hard to find and are prized among Dawn collectors.

Dawn also had a tremendous variety of extra clothing, and the following outfits are considered rare by collectors:

Furry Flurry: Blue and Green parka and pants.

Blues In the Night: A blue negligee.

Orange Blossom: A pair of baby doll pajamas and a matching robe.

Pink Panther: A pink satin gown with a silver coat.

The Blue "Chain Her Up" Outfit: This was a somewhat common outfit in red, but was a real rarity in blue. The box for this outfit varied as well.

Dawn's Dress Shop.
(Photo courtesy of Christine Gunderson.)

A wonderful find! Dawn's cars in their original packaging!
(Photo courtesy of Christine Gunderson.)

The Dawn and **Angie Head to Toe Dolls,** MIB. *(Photo courtesy of Katherine Burrows.)*

Collector's Advisory

Dawn's white tennis outfit, "What a Racket," when found in a tan version, is frequently being sold at the present time as a rarity—an unusual color variation. There are many experts, however, who believe that this is simply the more common white version that has oxidized to this tannish color. We have seen this type of oxidation in the Barbie line. Collectors would be well advised not to pay top dollar for this outfit until the controversy has been settled.

Dawn's Country Place: A new playset for Dawn was introduced in the 1972 Topper Toy Catalog, but there is much speculation among collectors as to whether or not it ever actually hit the market and was sold in stores. There were three different cardboard and vinyl rooms in this set, which came complete with furniture and a doll, and could be toted around by an attached handle. The Bedroom came with a bed, vanity and rocking chair. The Playroom came with a couch, chair and stereo. And the Patio set came with a barbecue, an umbrella table and a lounge chair.

Dawn's Pageant Cape: This was a send-in offer made through the purchase of Dawn's Beauty Pageant. Today, they are considered hard to find.

Head to Toe Dolls: These special Dawn Dolls came with three additional hairpieces, or "wiglets" as they were called, on the box—a long fall, ponytail, and a braid. They are very hard to find MIB.

DAWN UMBRELLA

Very hard to find is this Dawn kid-sized umbrella, which features Dawn, Glori, Jessica and Angie. Licensed by Topper and manufactured by Durham Industries, it was made in 1970. The author has located only two in the hands of collectors—one in yellow, and one in blue.

Dawn Umbrella.
(Photo courtesy of Christine Gunderson.)

Dawn Jewelry Boxes.
(Photo courtesy of Christine Gunderson.)

DAWN JEWELRY BOXES

These Dawn Jewelry Boxes feature a picture of Dawn and the name "Dawn" on their tops. One has a spinning ballerina; the other a spinning flower. Both are musical and are hard to find.

DAWN STORE DISPLAYS

Considered a real find is this original Dawn Store Display which features Dawn, Glori, Dale, Angie, Longlocks, Jessica, Ron, Van and Gary. This display was meant to promote the new line of Dancing Dawn Family dolls.

Dancing Dawn Family Dolls Store Display.
(Photo courtesy of Christine Gunderson.)

Recent issue of **Sugar Plum Fairy.**
(Photo by the author.)

EFFANBEE RARITIES

he firm of Fleischaker and Baum (F&B), began manufacturing dolls in 1910. After World War I, a "cold war" of sorts was waged against European toy manufacturers, and the American public stopped buying dolls and other toys from foreign shores. This gave American doll companies such as Effanbee an opportunity to prosper, and the following years, especially from 1920 to 1940, are known to avid Effanbee collectors as the "golden years." However, all of the dolls produced by Effanbee up to the present exhibit a high standard of quality and have a special charm and beauty.

Some of their most notable dolls over the years have been the Mama Doll—1923; Baby Grumpy—1924; Patsy—1927 (reissued in 1995); Honey—1952; Dy-Dee Baby—1956; Mickey—1959; Fluffy—1950s; Caroline—1970s; and the Bobsey Twins—1982. Also of special note was their 1930s line of portrait dolls by Dewees Cochran—the first realistically proportioned character dolls ever mass produced in the United States. These dolls by Mrs. Cochran are unsurpassed for their breath-taking beauty and incredible resemblance to real children.

Some memorable limited edition Effanbees were made during the 1970s and 1980s, and distributed by certain retailers. Retailers known by the author to have had these limited editions dolls were:

Shirley's Dollhouse: of Wheeling, Illinois. This is a large doll store and mail order business, very familiar to collectors across the country.

Treasure Trove: A large mail-order business started out of a garage in New York City during the 1950s, which grew to notable proportions and operated successfully for over 30 years. It was owned by Audrey and Martin Wank of Manhassett, New York, who were close associates of Roy Raizen, President and founder of Effanbee. In Mrs. Wank's recollection, there were at least ten limited editions, which included a Currier & Ives Boy and Girl Skater, a Grande Dame named Lorraine, a Southern Belle, and a Bride. *All of the limited editions from the Treasure Trove were Black dolls and were limited to a production of no more than 600 dolls.*

Bea's Dolls: This was a doll business owned and operated by Bea Skydell of Middlesex, New Jersey, but no additional information is available.

The hardest to find Effanbee dolls are, of course, the ones limited to a production of 600 or less. These distinguished issues are true "sleepers" right now. Rarely is one even seen advertised for sale, as the current Barbie

"Fluffy," by Effanbee.

1982 Bobbsey Twin dolls by Effanbee.
(Photos by the author.)

frenzy is consuming so much collector time and attention. They must, however, be in the "never to be forgotten" category, as they are simply too beautiful and rare to be written off. As the pendulum swings, these dolls should receive more of the recognition they deserve in the future. Now is an excellent time to start collecting Effanbees dolls that are 10 to 30 years old. Prices are currently quite low, especially for dolls of this high quality.

Other stores or companies that sold at least one limited edition Effanbee doll in this same time frame include:

- ◆ The Smithsonian Institution
- ◆ Meyer's (New Jersey)
- ◆ Sanger-Harris (Texas)
- ◆ The Winterbrook Corporation
- ◆ The Bear Creek Company (Oregon)

- ◆ Carson Pirie Scott (Illinois)
- ◆ Foley's (Texas)
- ◆ Gimbel's (New York)
- ◆ Amway

Anyone owning any of these limited editions (with the production limited to 600 or less) is encouraged to send along photographs to the author, in care of the publisher. What a great thing it would be to document all of these very special dolls!

Only 500 of these thirteen-inch **Annabelle Black Bride** dolls were made for the Treasure Trove in Manhasset, New York, in 1983. *(Photo by the author.)*

OTHER EFFANBEE RARITIES

An extremely limited edition of 125 dolls was produced of a Black version of the "Saratoga" doll of the Grande Dames Collection, made for the Treasure Trove in 1981. She is just like the white version in a black and white striped dress and bonnet, with a tulle veil covering her face. She is a very stylish and striking doll.

Another Effanbee rarity is a twenty-inch hard plastic Black boy doll made in 1951, and called, appropriately, "Black Little Boy." He had a lamb's wool wig (karakul, or caracul), bib overalls, a plaid shirt, a side-brimmed hat, and bare feet. He has very dark skin and sleep eyes. A most unique little guy, he is marked "EFFANBEE" on his head and back.

Jem Rarities

I spent quite a bit of time in the student lounge of Marquette University Law School in the mid-eighties. This is where I would meet my husband after he had spent an afternoon doing research at the Law Library. There was always that rare occasion when he'd be on schedule, but most of the time, research being as time consuming as it is, I'd spend at least an hour sitting around, listening to the law students speaking in legalese about patent infringement, torts, and other non-doll subjects. Those hours were long. But an amazing phenomena occurred each day at the same time: all conversation stopped as the Jem cartoon show appeared on the lounge TV, and quite a number of these bright, sophisticated young law students gathered around the set to watch. Jem actually seemed to have a larger pull than General Hospital—even during the time that Robin was dating an alien. That is one of the truly amazing things about the persona and themes that revolved around Jem—they were both intelligent enough and campy enough to capture the interest of adults.

The Original Misfits, Jem's rival band: From left to right, **Roxy, Pizzazz** and **Stormer.**

The Story of Jem

The character of Jem, born "Jerrica," had a scientist father, a singer mother, and a sister named Kimber. Before their parents untimely deaths, the father had invented a computer that could create holograms, and the mother founded the Starlight Foundation, which was a foster home for young girls. When Jerrica (Jem) and her sister Kimber decided to start a rock band, two of the foster girls from their mother's Starlight Foundation—Aja and Shana—were invited to join. Jerrica acquired a pair of star-shaped earrings that could control her father's computer, named Snergy, through her own voice commands. The computer could be used to create holograms for their performances, and ultimately, was used to transform Jerrica into Jem. Many of the show's themes revolved

First Issue Jem and the Holograms. From left to right, **Shana, Aja, Jem** and **Kimber.**

The Starlight Girls (from the home for girls that Jem runs). From left to right, **Ashley, Krissie** and **Banee.**

Second year Misfits, Jetta and **Clash.**

around the girls trying to keep Snergy a secret, for fear that it could be used for untold evil if it fell into the wrong hands.

Rio, a male character, was Jerrica's childhood sweetheart, and, as an adult, found himself in love with both Jerrica and Jem, never realizing they were the same person. Sort of a cartoon-male version of Lois Lane.

The character of Jem, as well as her rock group known as the Holograms, were very moral, loving people. The two sisters kept their mother's foundation for homeless girls alive and always strove to do the right thing. The downfall of the show came from the viewing parents' concern over the violence surrounding the Hologram's rival group, the Misfits, and the show's eventual tie-in with MTV—a most questionable tie-in for any show targeted for young children.

The Jem family dolls made by Hasbro during the 1980s are well made and notably unique and innovative. They also did something that few other dolls could boast about: for periods of time, they outsold Barbie! A lot of parents, myself included, feel that if the show's producers had only stayed away from the promotion of MTV to the children watching the show, both the program and the dolls would have enjoyed continued success, as there was quite a bit of quality and substance in the very foundation of the storylines and themes.

SOME JEM JEOGRAPHY

Emmet Benton . . . . Jem's scientist father

Jacqui Benton . . . . Jem's singer mother

Jerrica Benton . . . . Jem's original name

Kimber Benton . . . . Jem's sister

Snergy . . . . Emmet Benton's invention, a
computer that could create holograms.

Aja Leith &
  Shana Elmsferg . . . . The first foster girls to be taken in by Jacqui.

Holograms . . . . Rock band formed by Jem which included
herself, sister Kimber, Shana and Aja.

Raya (Carmen Alonso),

Danse (Giselle Divorjack) &

Video (Vivien Montgomery) . . . . . Three new members to the group,
Holograms, that were added the second
year.

Rio Pacheco . . . . Jem's (Jerrica's) childhood sweetheart,
now the Hologram's stage manager.

Pizzazz (Phyllis Gabor),

Stormer (Mary Phillips) &

Roxy (Roxanne Pellegrini) . . . . . . First year members of the nasty rival
group, the Misfits.

Jetta (Sheila Thompson) . . . . Second year addition to Misfits, from
Britain.

Clash
  (Constance Montgomery) . . . . . . Misfit wannabee, also Video's cousin.

Starlight Girls:
  Banee, Krissie & Ashley . . . . From the foster home for girls that Jem
now runs since the death of her mother,
the original director.

All told, there were twenty-four Jem family dolls made, most of which came with a cassette tape and poster. There were about 60 fashions, and a variety of playsets including two Jaguars with working FM radios, a star stage, a dressing room, a waterbed, and even a radio station with a working microphone!

The entire line of Jem dolls and accessories are to be commended for their innovations and creativity. They are slowly becoming more collectible each successive year.

RARITY

**Second Issue
Shana** and **Aja.**
*(Photo courtesy of
Rick Conlon.)*

Second Issue Shana and Aja

The second issue of Shana, (left) shown here mint in box, is considered rare, and the second issue of Aja, (right), also shown MIB, is considered hard to find. Shana and Aja were orphaned girls in Jem's mother's Starlight Foundation Foster Home, who later joined Jem's rock band, the Holograms. Like most Jem family dolls, each came with an audio cassette featuring the music of the Holograms.

Jem Mail-in Premiums

The Jem Pet Llama and the Jem MTV Jacket were mail-in premiums and are now considered hard to find. Jem's tie-in with MTV was considered by many as a demonstration of incredibly poor judgment on the part of her producers, and probably led to the show's downfall.

RARE AND HARD-TO-FIND JEM FASHIONS

Jem's fashions **"She Makes an Impression"** (left), **"Moroccan Magic"** (center) and **"Getting Down to Business"** (right) are all considered hard to find. *(Photo courtesy of Rick Conlon.)*

Rio's outfit **"Share a Little Bit"** (left), and Jem's outfit **"Running With the Wind"** (center) are both considered rare. Rio's outfit **"Rappin"** (right) is considered hard to find. *(Photo courtesy of Rick Conlon.)*

Glitter 'N Gold Jem stands next to **Rio,** her childhood sweetheart, who is wearing a rare Truly Outrageous Outfit: the black tux. *(Photo courtesy of Rick Conlon.)*

Kindergarten Kathy.
(Photo by Author.)

HORSMAN RARITIES

The Horsman Company was founded in the mid-1800s in New York City by Edward Horsman. Creators of the "grotesque" Billiken, they forged a name for themselves by the early 1900s. Mr. Horsman had a special knack for turning a penny on whatever were the popular trends of the day.

Over the years, the Horsman Company continued to capitalize on current rages. They had their own version of Shirley Temple, Tiny Tears, Patty Playpal, Ideal's Pepper, Liddle Kiddles, Effanbee's Fluffy, and so on.

The Horsman dolls of the early 1950s, particularly, were gorgeous. With lots of lustrous hair, sweet kissable faces, and frilly little dresses, they set afloat many a happy childhood memory among the battalions of Baby Boomers who got to play with them.

It was during this time that Horsman developed two innovative new materials for the manufacture of dolls: Fairy Skin, noted for its realistic "feel"; and Softee Skin, another realistic material which was also pliable. Both gave an extra measure of success to an already strong company.

Considered a staple in the world of dolls, Horsman has always provided the American public with a less costly alternative to the "must-haves" on children's wish lists and with a variety of solid, well-made play dolls.

Two **"Ruthies"**: examples of some of the popular, mass-produced Horsman dolls of the '50s and '60s. *(Photo by the author.)*

A more recent example of the **Black Ruthie doll,** considered hard to find.

'50s & '60s Horsman Dolls

The older Horsman dolls are gorgeous, and need more recognition! The following is a list of the Horsman dolls from the 1950s and 1960s that are, today, the hardest to find. If anyone owns one of these dolls, please send along photos and information to the author, in care of the publisher.

<u>Year</u>	<u>Doll</u>
1959	25-inch Wonderful Baby
1950	Playmate Dolls (boy and girl set)
1952	25-inch Rosebud
1953	Shadow Wave Doll (with complete kit)
1961	Jackie
1961-62	Jackie Bride
1966	Patty Duke with Record
1967	36-inch Cindy
1952	Black Tynie Baby
1953	Black Doll
1951	Softee Doll with Fur Wig
1953	White Tynie Baby in Christening Gown
1954	Black Fairy Skin Baby
1955	Cindy Strutter (with complete wardrobe case)
1956	Black Bride
1956-57	Black Baby Precious
1956	Black Polly and Pete (black twins)
1959	Black Peggy Ann
	Any Black Softee Baby
1960	Peggy Ann Bride (with or without complete wardrobe case)
	White Princess Peggy
	Black Princess Peggy
1960	Fantastic Ruthie with Lotion
	Black Baby Buttercup
1961	Black Walk-A-Bye
	Mary Poppins Gift Set with Extra Clothes (MIB, with either adult or little girl doll as Mary Poppins)
1966	36-inch Alice in Wonderland
	Baby Grow-Up (with all parts)
1966	Christopher Robin and Pooh
1966	Mary Poppins, Michael and Jane Set (MIB)
1966	Michael and Jane Set (MIB)
1966	Large Mary Poppins
1967	Mary Poppins Umbrella
1968	Raggedy Ann Umbrella

DOLL BUGGY RARITIES

*A*h, the springtimes of childhood! Each heralded day brings more hours of sunshine, warmer breezes and more playtime! Get out the lightweight sweaters, the baseball bats, the kites, and of course, our dearly beloved doll buggies. Some of my own earliest childhood memories are of pushing my doll buggy endlessly around the back parking lot of our Kenmore Street apartment building in Chicago. This was an activity that filled me with a blissful type of contentment that I never seemed to tire of. There are likely quite a number in my generation who can relate to that feeling, because just like the children of the Baby Boom era themselves, our dolls were also provided for like no generation before us. Every doll accessory and accouterment imaginable found its way on to the market for doting post-WWII parents to snatch up for us. It has been said that we had more toys and more time to play with them than any other generation in history.

(Photo by the author.)

A **seventeen-inch Shirley Temple** in a vintage, late 1950s unmarked doll buggy. *(Photo by the author.)*

By all accounts, it seems that Joel Ellis of Springfield, Vermont made the very first baby carriages in America, in the mid-1800s. His "perambulators," as the were called, became so popular that he started to fashion scaled-down carriages for dolls from leftover scrap material. His 1866 catalog shows a three-wheel doll carriage with a padded seat and a large canopy-style hood. The price at the time was $17.50 per dozen. Some 3,262 of them were sold in the first season. A smaller version of this very first American doll buggy was fashioned for smaller dolls and 8,676 of them were sold during the first year for $8 a dozen.

Quite a number of generic doll buggies have been manufactured in the years since, providing many an American child with many an hour logged on cloud nine. Their popularity seemed to reach its peak in the postwar era, before women's lib, when the nicest thing you could say about a girl's toy was that it was "just like Mommy's." But, even today, many are sold and enjoyed. Certain Baby Boom dolls such as Chatty Cathy, Chatty Baby, Suzie Cute by Deluxe Reading, Madame Alexander's Dionne Quintuplets, and Shirley Temple had doll buggies manufactured specifically for them.

There are also some novelty doll buggies from the era for the collector to search out. In Mattel's hugely popular Liddle Kiddle family, both Florence Niddle (the nurse Kiddle) and Baby Liddle had their own buggies—each bringing top dollar on today's collector's market. Barbie's littlest sister from the mid-1960s, Tutti, had a doll buggy as part of her "Walkin' My Dolly" playset. The pram-style carriage came with a tiny plastic baby and bunting. Suzie Cute by Deluxe Reading had a carriage fashioned specifically for her—a multi-colored plastic affair with the colorful plastic disks that were the trademark of her accessories. Nancy Flatsy, dressed as an English nanny, came with an ornate pram for her to push with a miniature Flatsy doll inside.

And the list can go on and on . . . with all the fuss and fanfare made over the dolls themselves, not enough is heard about the accessories, such as these beloved buggies that make the dolls so much more fun to play with and contribute so generously to happy childhood memories!

Chatty Cathy's Walk and Talk Stroller.
(Photo courtesy of Ruth Kibbons.)

Shirley Temple Buggy.
(Photo courtesy of Patricia Snyder.)

CHATTY CATHY'S WALK AND TALK STROLLER

Very hard to find and very sought after by the legions of Chatty collectors is Chatty Cathy's Walk and Talk Stroller. It was quite a novelty, as it had a remote control mechanism that allowed the "little mother" to prompt Chatty to speak by pulling a ring on the stroller's handle that attached to the doll's own pullstring. It had a tubular steel frame, with a vinyl seat and fringed canopy.

ORIGINAL SHIRLEY TEMPLE BUGGIES

This original Shirley Temple doll buggy is a true rarity on today's collector's market. Made originally in the 1930s to compliment the Shirly Temple Baby doll by Ideal, small quantities of them may have been manufactured through the '40s and possibly into the early '50s. Made of a natural color wicker, it is a pram-style carriage with a hood and a Shirley Temple medallion on its side. I feel that, beause of their strudiness, many more of these buggies may have survived the years than what we are currently aware of, but are presently unidentified because the medallions have fallen off.

Chatty Baby's Nine-Way Stroller Buggy

Extremely hard to find, especially with all of its parts, is this nine-way stroller buggy, made for Chatty Baby, which is actually a very versatile collection of interchangeable pieces. There were five pieces in all that could be mixed and matched in nine different ways. There was a metal stroller frame with wheels, a glider frame that could rock, an A-frame that made a baby swing, a car seat, and a car bed.

Chatty Baby's Nine-Way Stroller Buggy in it's glider frame.
(Photo by Kent Gunther.)

Nine-Way Stroller Buggy as a car seat.
(Photo by Kent Gunther.)

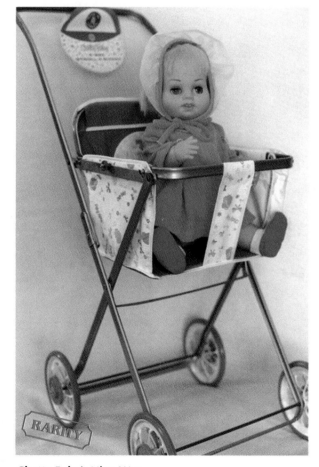

Chatty Baby's Nine-Way Stroller Buggy as a stroller.
(Photo courtesy of Beth Gunther.)

PAPER DOLL RARITIES

olls have always been unique in the world of toys because of the maternal and paternal feelings they engender in children and because of the opportunity they afford for play-acting at life. Paper dolls are unique in the world of dolls because by their very nature, whether store bought or drawn at the kitchen table, they have been accessible to almost all children, regardless of family income. From their start as toy books in the early 1800s to their current celebration of today's top selling dolls, they have also given us valuable insight into our history.

From **Queen Holden's "Baby Shower"** which featured seven baby dolls, and wonderful outfits and accessories. *(Photo by the author.)*

155

TOY BOOKS

In 1810, England gave birth to a new and innovative plaything called "toy books," which contained paper figures of children, flowers, landscapes, etc., and also provided a story line. Children could use their imaginations with these little paper models and create their own scenarios, or follow the story line presented in the book. In their time, toy books were hugely popular and went through numerous printings.

Because there were no foreign copyright laws to speak of, two American printers—J. Belcher of Boston and William Charles of Philadelphia—were able to capitalize on the enormous popularity of these toy books by simply copying them. The very first of these was a small book in a cardboard slipcase called *The History of Little Fanny Exemplified in a Series of Figures*, printed by S.& J. Fuller of London.

EUROPEAN BOXED DOLLS

Toward the mid-1800s, paper dolls manufactured in Europe and packaged in elaborately decorated boxes, began being bought up by America's wealthier families. They were beautifully and painstakingly made, quite costly, and quite different from today's counterparts. The detail evidenced in the drawings demonstrates the high standards of the artists who drew them. The outlines of these drawings were far more complicated for children to cut out than what we are familiar with today. Lace and scalloped edging on the clothing, along with tiny ribbons and accessories, presented a real challenge to the young ones of that era who were routinely taught needlework and handwork at an early age.

Some of the common characteristics of these European boxed paper dolls are: (1) two identical dolls appearing within the set; (2) costumes vividly hand colored, painted with lacquer for protection, and with both front and back views included; and (3) beautiful, well-made boxes to house the doll and her outfits. The boxes were elegantly decorated and detailed and the sets' titles were printed in more than one language, as so many of these sets were exported all over the world. Many of the dolls in these boxed sets came with gilt metal stands.

Many collectors believe that the European boxed paper dolls from this era are the most coveted and sought after in the arena of paper dolls, as well as the most expensive.

THE FIRST AMERICAN PAPER DOLLS

Although not as elaborate as their European equivalents, the first American paper dolls, which appeared around 1854, were purchased regularly and roundly loved. The first known American paper doll was Fanny Gray, manufactured by Cosby, Nichols & Company of Boston. The story line consisted of the ups and downs of this little orphan, who finds her way to a lost relative. Her costumes were typical of the day, and her popularity gave vent to many more American paper dolls that were to follow. Other popular figures were Charley, Alice, and Little Fairy Lightfoot, by Chandler; Cousin Charles aand the May Queen, by Dubois; Mother, Father, Little Brother, Baby, and Miss Adelaid, by Anson Randolph; and Clara West, Susie's Pet and Sarah Brown, by McLoughlin. Less expensive than these fancy boxed sets were sets that came in decorated envelopes. Between 1850-1900 paper doll sets, depending on size, usually sold for between a penny and fifteen cents.

The Gilded Age
1870-1900

The Victorian era was an affluent one, as there were no income taxes and fortunes were easier to accumulate. Just as with parlor games, the production of paper dolls, both in this country and abroad, increased as there was more industrial capability to produce them and more leisure time to command them. Small scissors were now affordable to most everyone, and prices on the paper doll sets themselves had dropped to the point where they, too, were accessible to many more families. Little girls, more adept at handwork than today's children, created additional clothing for these prized paper dolls out of bits and scraps from their mother's sewing baskets.

Paper doll sets with cutesy-catchy names like Bessie Bliss, Polly Prim, Winsome Winnie, Merry Marion, and Dolly Dimple, lined the shelves of book stores and drawing rooms. Some of the dolls from this era were jointed at the shoulders and legs. The paper dolls in this time frame were produced in greater quantities and usually sold for between 5 to 15 cents per set.

Other popular sets of the time were: Lovely Lilly, Lordly Lionel, and Sweet Abigail, by Tuck; Baby Blue, Diane the Bride, and Mamie, by McLoughlin; and the many advertising paper dolls used to promote certain products such as Pillsbury Flour, Lion and McLaughlin Coffees, Diamond Dye, and Clark's Thread.

Turn of the Century

One of the significant signs of the end of the Victorian era was slowly rising hemlines. As it is usual for paper dolls to mimic the current fashion trends, these shorter hemlines were reflected in the paper dolls that were produced from 1910-1929, and can help collectors in dating their finds. Another earmark of the times was the introduction of the Teddy Bear (1903).

Some of the popular paper dolls of this period were: Teddy Bear and Lady Betty, by Selchow & Righter; Grace Green and Nellie North, by McLoughlin; and Sister Prue on Charles Street, by Polly's Paper Playmates. Some particularly enduring classics were introduced in this time frame—Kewpies by Rose O'Neill; Dolly Dingle, and Billy Bumps, created by Grace Drayton.

What could be considered the first paper doll series to represent movie stars was run in the publication, *Ladies World* from 1916-1918. Some of the stars featured were:

Mary Pickford . . . . September 1916

Billie Burke . . . . October 1916

George Le Guere . . . . March 1917

Charlie Chaplin . . . . July 1917

Paper dolls were becoming so popular that they were being printed on the backs of cereal boxes, food labels, and wrappers of various kinds; even tucked into sugar and tobacco sacks, and coffee and flour bags.

Paper houses also became popular during this period. Family homes, schools, and even entire villages were constructed out of sturdy cardboard, with the brick, windows, and exterior landscaping being drawn on.

Anne Tolstoi Wallach, author of the book *Paper Dolls* (Van Nostrand Reinhold, 1982) writes: "But probably the most important event of the period for paper dolls was the opening by F.W. Woolworth of the first of his stores with the familiar red and gold fronts . . . for the next 50 years American girls would make some of their most momentous decisions about which paper doll book to buy next with their pennies."

THE ROARING TWENTIES AND THE DAPPER THIRTIES

These were the most prolific years of paper doll production. Every little girl and her sister wanted a set. They were in their hey day.

Most indicative of the 1920s and 1930s in American paper dolls is the prevalence of celebrity and movie star themes. Movies were everywhere, even in small towns, and movie magazines helped to promote the fervor. Shirley Temple, Mary Pickford, Mary Miles Minter, Marguerite Clark, Lila Lee, Norma Talmadge, May Allison, Charlie Chaplin, Gerladine Farrar, Douglas Fairbanks, Jackie Coogan, the Our Gang cast, Baby Peggy, Claudette Colbert, Anita Page, and Clara Bow were just some of the celebrities to be honored in paper doll form during this era. Similarly honored were Sonja Henie, the Dionne Quintuplets, Baby Snooks, Charlie McCarthy, Olivia de Haviland, Ruby Keeler, Red Skelton, Kate Smith, Ida Lupino, Anita Louise, Spencer Tracy, Irene Dunne, James Cagney, Alice Faye, Norma Shearer, Charles Laughton, Fred Astaire, Rosalind Russel, Myrna Loy, Helen Hayes, Laurel and Hardy, and Jane Withers. The format, which was similar in many of these sets, offered a portrait doll of the star on the cover of the book—made of heavier paper stock and perforated, so that they could be pressed out. The inside pages included all of the costumes and various accessories such as furs, jewelry, corsages, tiaras, gloves, fans, shoes and bags. These costumes and accessories included all of the glamour and glitz you would expect of Hollywood and other celebrities of that era. The concept of celebrity paper dolls was so popular and well received by the public that they were even printed on the covers of school tablets.

Some of the popular comic strips of the time like the Katzenjammer Kids, Flash Gordon, Bringing up Father, and Winnie Winkle were also made into paper doll sets and they, too, were very much in demand.

One of the all time stars in paper doll design, Queen Holden, came into her own during this era. Truly a celebrity in her own right, she produced her first paper doll book, "Baby Joan," in 1929. Reprints of Queen Holden's gorgeous paper dolls became available again in the late 1980s.

On the whole, these were banner years for paper dolls. After all, what other item could a Depression-era child acquire for ten cents that would reward them with so many hours of enjoyment and fascination?

THE 1940s

The rumblings of WWII started in 1939, and the paper dolls of the 1940s very much reflected this. Girls in Uniform, Victory Paper Dolls, WACS & WAVES, Tom the Aviator, Dick the Sailor, and Harry the Soldier were some of the titles on paper doll sets that included full uniform changes and weapons among their pages.

One set in particular, manufactured by the Pachter Company in 1943, was titled Ten Beautiful Girls in Uniform and included "90 large pieces, 25 complete uniforms front and back, in full realistic colors, also history of girls in service." The set also engaged in a bit of promotion, listing the nine services open to women in WWII: the WACS, WAVES, WOWS, SPARS, Marines, Red Cross, Navy Nurses and WASPS.

Military cutouts for boys were also made available at this time, but the stereotype of paper dolls being a "girl thing" was too strong for these sets to become big sellers.

Also of course, hugely popular was the film *Gone With the Wind*. The novel came first, in 1936, and sales were still going strong in 1947, replacing Uncle Tom's Cabin as the number one all-time best seller. The firm started shooting in 1939, and the Merrill Company was commissioned to create the paper doll sets to tie in with the movie. The costumes in the Merrill paper doll sets replicated the film's costumes in every detail and are prized acquisitions for the serious paper doll collector.

Other movie star and celebrity paper doll sets continued to be popular during this period. Nearly every notable film star became a paper doll in the 1940s. Titles on the best seller list in the '40s included the likes of Judy Garland, Deanna Durbin, Betty Grable, Tyrone Power, Linda Darnell, Jeanette MacDonald, Bob Hope, Dorothy Lamour, Glan Miller, Benny Goodman, Rita Hayworth, Hedy Lamarr, Lana Turner, Betty Davis, and Bing Crosby.

THE BABY BOOM ERA

After WWII, no one wanted to look at military uniforms anymore. People had "done without" and "made do" long enough and a bit of extravagance was back in style.

For the children of the Baby Boom era, every toy, doll and doll accessory imaginable lined the shelves of toy stores and sang out their jingles via television commercials imploring doting post-WWII parents to grab for them.

The "all-American-girl-next-door" made her debut, and stars like Annette Funicello and Sandra Dee replaced the glamour and glitz types from a decade before.

And of course, no one can ignore the powerful force of that tiny flickering box in the living room. Television hit the scene, followed by rave reviews. Between 1948 and 1958, over 15 billion American dollars were spent on TV sets. Both television and the movies, and their corresponding publicity campaigns, were becoming a big part of American culture. Following suit, some of the top selling paper dolls of the era were based on suchs personalities and shows as "I Love Lucy," "Mary Hartline," "The Honeymooners," "Ozzie and Harriet," Roy Rogers and Dale Evans, Rock Hudson, Elizabeth Taylor, Sandra Dee, "My Little Margie," Natalie Wood, Diana Lynn, and Eve Arden.

Others included Loretta Young, The Lennon Sisters, The Mouseketeers, June Allyson, Grace Kelly, Captain Kangaroo, "Kookie" Byrnes, "Hawaiian Eye," Donna Reed, Pat Boone, Debbie Reynolds, Doris Day, and Dr. Kildare.

Not be overlooked were Marilyn Monroe, Kim Novak, Twiggy, Pat & Tricia Nixon, Dennis the Menace, Shari Lewis and her puppets, Patty Duke, Elly May Clampett, "The Beverly Hillbillies," and "Petticoat Junction."

And, of course, there is always "Lassie," "The Munsters," Tabitha (from "Bewitched"), "Green Acres," "That Girl," Buffy (from "Family Affair"), "The Flying Nun," Julia, Mary Poppins, Tuesday Weld, Haley Mills, and "Laugh-In."

The Wendy Ann Series.
(Photo by the author.)

Many of the covers of these paper doll sets opened up in unique ways and "statuette" dolls were created which were glossy and more substantial, being made of double-weight cardboard.

Another popular draw were the top-selling dolls of the Baby Boom era. Ever-eager Baby Boomers made dolls like Shirley Temple, Chatty Cathy (the first mass-produced talking doll, made by Mattel in 1960), Little Kiddles (tiny dolls with big personalities, also made by Mattel in the '60s), Wendy Ann (an eight-inch Madame Alexander masterpiece with a drop-dead wardrobe), Raggedy Ann (a true classic born in 1918 and still in demand in the '50s and '60s), and of course, Barbie—some of the most popular dolls in history. All of these Baby Boom favorites and many more have paper counterparts.

BETSY MCCALL

In the mid-1800s, a very well-received fashion magazine for women, called *Godey's Lady's Book* came up with a brilliant idea. It occurred to Mr. Godey that his magazine could better serve its readers if it included a page or two to occupy the young children of its adult readers, while they were themselves engaged in reading the publication. It followed, therefore, that among the pages of sewing patterns, household hints and recipes were logically tucked a few pages of paper dolls to amuse the youngsters while their mothers read in peace. This was the very first magazine paper doll, followed in later years by a caravan of others, including Betty Bonnet, Lettie Lane, and an all-time Baby Boom favorite, Betsy McCall.

Betsy McCall premiered in *McCall's* magazine in May of 1951 and she had a parade of curtain calls leading right up to 1974. Her clothing and activities, through the years, reflected society at the time. She was distinctive in that she was a brown-haired doll, standing out in a sea of blondes. She gave the countless numbers of brunette children of the era someone to relate to. The Betsy McCall paper doll pages showed her growing up, celebrating holidays, becoming a foster parent to a sponsored child, fighting pollution, raising money for UNICEF, and just plain playing in the sandbox (to name a few activities). She was recreated successfully in real doll form many times, and is a real darling among collectors.

Specialties Du Jour

Currently, Peck Gandre is to be applauded for their wonderful execution of such classics as Jacqueline (Kennedy), Little Women, Wendy Ann (Madame Alexander), Scarlett, Barbie series, Cinderella, Snow White, Alice in Wonderland, Dorothy visits Oz, Bru Jane, Hilda Toddler, Mein Liebling, and many more. These exquisite paper doll sets are presently available.

Collecting Hints

1. As paper ages, it produces acid. Acid-free storage folders can be purchased at library supply stores.

2. When mounting paper dolls in albums or picture frames, they should be placed against an acid-free backing, such as Poly-C or acid free Mylar.

3. Just as with old books, paper dolls should be kept away from humidity, as mold could form.

4. Where to find them? Rummage sales, flea markets and second-hand stores are still wonderful sources. Non-collectors put very little value on a set of paper dolls, so they can still be picked up for a song. For the older sets, antique stores and antique malls, collectors' ads, and the occasional doll show can yield a lot of finds.

5. Things to look for: Uncut sets are always worth more than those that have been cut. Permanent markings such as crayon or ink, rips, bent corners, and dolls with bent necks, wrists and ankles, all detract from the set's value.

Peck-Gandre's "Hilda Toddler"
paper doll.

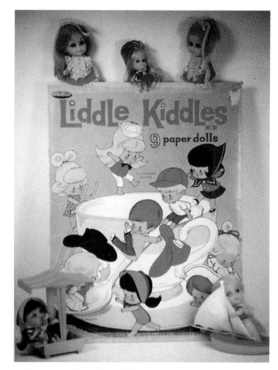

**Whitman's "Liddle Kiddles—
9 paper dolls"**

More examples of
Queen Holden's warm,
sensitive art work.
(Photo by the author.)

Over the last 180 years, paper dolls have not only offered children count-less hours of immersion and enjoyment, but have also given us an irreplace-able history of fashion, celebrities, and the customs of each given era. So cherished have they been, whether store bought or home drawn, that many still survive from a century ago, complete with their perfect faces, elegant wardrobes, and still covered with tiny finger prints.

Two of **Queen Holden's toddlers.**
(Photo by the author.)

VALUES

All values are approximate and will vary according to area of the country. You will see similar values among paper dolls sets from the same decade dealing with the same subject matter (such as movie stars from the '40s, TV shows from the '60s, and so forth). Values on paper dolls based on the older television programs seem to rise a bit when the series is featured on "Nick at Nite."

But, remember! Regardless of the values listed here, paper dolls are one of those unique collectibles that may still be picked up for pocket change at church rummage sales, neighborhood garage sales, and second-hand stores like St. Vincent De Paul and Salvation Army, because they are held in very little esteem by non-collectors.

Sets considered rare when found in uncut condition.

The following are only examples from various eras:

Annette Funicello, Whitman 1958 (EX) $30.00

Archies, 1969 (near mint) 25.00

All Star Movie Cut-Outs, Whitman 1934 (mint) 80.00

Ava Gardner, #965 Whitman 1949 (mint) .50.00

Ann Blyth, #2550 Merrill 1953 (mint) 40.00

Angela Cartwright, #4101 Transogram 1961 . . . . .25.00

Baby Nancy, #W966 Whitman 1935 (EX) .55.00

Baby Tenderlove, #1949 Whitman (near mint) 12.00

Bette Davis, Merrill 1942 (EX) 45.00

Betty Grable, #962 Whitman 1946 (mint) $60.00

Bob Hope & Dorothy Lamour, #976 Whitman 1942 (mint) 60.00

Bob Cummings Fashion Models, #2732 Bonnie

Brooks, 1958 (mint) 30.00

Beverly Hillbillies, #1955 Whitman 1964 (mint) 20.00

Bewitched, #144 Magic Wand 1965 (mint) 25.00

Claudette Colbert, #2451 Saalfield 1943 (EX) 44.00

(mint) 60.00

Carmen Miranda, #995 Whitman 1942 (mint) 60.00

Cyd Charisse, #2084 Whitman 1956 (mint) 40.00

Caroline Kennedy, #109 Magic Wand (mint) 20.00

Connie Francis, #1956 Whitman 1963 (mint) 20.00

Dionne Quints Cut-Outs, 1930s (EX+) .99.00

Dionne Quints, #M3404 Merrill 1936 (EX+) 45.00

(mint) 99.00

Deanna Durbin, #3480 Merrill 1940 (mint) 60.00

Deanna Durbin, #4804 Merrill 1941 (mint) 60.00

Dinah Shore, #977 Whitman 1943 (mint) 60.00

Dinah Shore, #2060 Whitman 1956 (mint) 40.00

Doris Day, #s 1179, 1952, 1977, 2103, Whitman 1950s (mint) each . .40.00

Dennis the Menace (Jay North), #1991 Whitman 1960 (mint) 20.00

Donna Reed, #2743 Saalfield 1961 . . . . .20.00

Elizabeth Taylor Cut-Outs, Whitman 1950s (near mint) 45.00

Elizabeth Taylor, #968 Whitman 1949 (mint) 50.00

Elizabeth Taylor, #s 2048, 1177, 1193, 1951, 2057, 2112

Whitman 1950s (mint) each 40.00

Elly May, #1819 Watkins 1963 (mint) .15.00

Family Affair, #4767 Whitman 1968 (mint) 15.00

Flying Nun, #5131 Saalfield 1968 (mint) 15.00

Glamour Models, #177 Stevens 1960s (mint) 2.00

Gone With the Wind, #3404 1940 (near mint) 350.00

Gone With the Wind, #3405 Merrill 1940 (Ex) 200.00

Greer Garson, #4848 Merrill 1944 (mint) 60.00

Grace Kelly, #2049, #2609 Whitman 1958 & 1959 (mint) 40.00

Gidget (Sally Field), #601 Standard 1961 (mint) 15.00

Green Acres, #1979 & #4773 Whitman 1962 & 1967 (mint) 15.00

Happy Kids, #775 & #275 Burton 1935 (near mint) 50.00

Hollywood Fashion Dolls, #2242 Saalfield (EX) 35.00

Hollywood Personalities, #L1049 Lowe 1941 (mint) 60.00

Hayley Mills, #1955 & #1960 Whitman 1965 & 1964 (mint) 15.00

John Wayne, 1981 (mint) 10.00

Jane Withers, Dell #1938, Whitman #977 & #996

1936 & 1938 (mint) each about 80.00

Judy Garland, #980, #996 & #999 Whitman 1940s (mint) $60.00

Janet Lennon, #1956 & #1964 Whitman 1956 & 1958 (mint) each
   about 30.00

Janet Lennon, #1948 & #4613 Whitman 1961 & 62 (mint) each 20.00

Lennon Sisters, #1991 Whitman 1959 (mint) . . . . .30.00 to 65.00

Lucille Ball, Saalfield 1945 (near mint) 65.00

Lucille Ball with Desi Arnez, #2101 Whitman 1953 (mint) 50.00

Lucille Ball with Desi Arnez and Little Ricky, #2116
   Whitman 1953 (mint) 50.00

Lucy, #1963 & #4610 Whitman 1964 & 63 (mint) 20.00

Lana Turner, #964, #975, & #988 Whitman 1940s (mint) each
   about 60.00

Laugh-In, #1325 Saalfield 1969 . . . . .12.00

Marilyn Monroe, Saalfield 1954 (VG) 166.00

Mary Poppins, 1966 (mint) 40.00

Margaret O'Brien, #963, #964, & #970 Whitman
   1940s (mint) each 60.00

Mouseketeers Cut-Outs, #1974 Whitman 1957 (mint) 30.00

My Little Margie, #2737 Whitman 1954 (mint) 40.00

Pat Boone, #1968 Whitman 1959 (near mint) . . . . .30.00 to 75.00

Princess Paper Doll Book, #2216 Saalfield 1939 (mint) 70.00

Patti Page, #2406 & #2488 Lowe 1957 & 1958 (mint) 30.00

Patty Duke, Whitman 1960s (mint) 25.00

Petticoat Junction, #1954 Whitman 1964 (mint) 20.00

Pollyanna (Haley Mills), Golden Press 1960 (mint) 20.00

Pebbles & Bamm-Bamm, Whitman 1965 (mint) 43.00

Pebbles Flintstone, #1997 Whitman 1960s (mint) 45.00

Rock Hudson, #2087 Whitman 1957 (near mint) . . . . .30.00 to 60.00

Ricky Nelson, #2081 Whitman 1959 (mint) 30.00

Roy Rogers, several by Whitman, 1950s (mint)
   each . . . . .45.00 to 60.00

Shirley Temple, several by Saalfield 1930s (EX to mint)
   each . . . . .90.00 and 150.00

Shirley Temple, #6032 Saalfield 1958 (mint) 45.00

Shirley Temple, #301 Gabriel 1961 (mint) 25.00

Sonja Henie, #3475 Merrill 1939 (mint) 75.00

Spanky and Darla, #2759 Saalfield 1957 .35.00

Tabatha ("Bewitched"), #115, Magic Wand 1966 (mint) 25.00

Twiggy, #1999 Whitman 1967 (mint) 20.00

Wedding of the Paper Dolls, #3497 Merrill 1935 (EX) 60.00

Zorro (Guy Williams), Aldon 1960s 20.00

TERRI LEE IN 3-D PAPER DOLLS

This is an extremely hard to find paper doll set. Made of rigid vinyl, the doll and her outfits were "puffed" out from the base card that they were attached to, giving a 3-D effect. Made in 1954, stock #6657, the set included a cowgirl outfit, a confirmation or communion dress, a majorette costume, a suit, party dresses and more. This set sold originally for $2.95.

Close-up shot of the **"Terri Lee 3-D paper dolls,"** with an example of the 3-D doll figure. The box reads: "The world's best dressed doll in sensational 3-Dimensional cut-outs. Made of durable plastic in beautiful 'Terri Color.' " *(Photo courtesy of Joy Crawford.)*

TAMMY AND HER FAMILY

Tammy collectors agree that this set of five paper dolls, which includes Tammy, her mom and dad, and her brother and sister, are extremely hard to find. The set included all punch-outs and two room settings as backdrops.

A Note on Paper Doll Rarities

There are certain sets within a series or line of paper dolls (such as Barbie paper dolls and Chatty paper dolls) that are harder to find than the other sets in that line. However, please keep in mind that any older paper doll set that is found in uncut condition is a rarity. Paper dolls during the modern doll era—from about 1945 to the present—have always been the kind of items that were purchased to be immediately put in the hands of children, and used. They weren't meant to sit up on a shelf for display, or to be tucked way for a special occasion. They had to be cut in order to be used. A harder to find set that is found in uncut condition is additionally rare.

Tammy and Her Family paper doll. *(Photo courtesy of Linda Ladd.)*

Charmin's
Activity Book.

Chatty Cathy Tote
Bag Paper Dolls.

CHATTY CATHY TOTE BAG PAPER DOLLS

Considered hard-to-find is this 1961 Whitman cut-out set, which featured 45 costumes and accessories.

CHARMIN'S ACTIVITY BOOK

Hard to find among Charmin Chatty's paper doll sets is this activity book, which featured Charmin at a western ranch.

Liddle Kiddles
Storybook Sweethearts.

LIDDLE KIDDLES STORYBOOK SWEETHEARTS

Also considered hard-to-find is this 1969 Whitman set which featured eight paper dolls and their clothes.

A group of **Waltons Paper Dolls.** (*Courtesy of the J. Lawrence Collection.*)

WALTONS PAPER DOLLS

Another hard-to-find 1970s paper doll set is the one pictured here, at center. Made by Whitman (stock #1995) in 1975, it is flanked by a Waltons Little Golden Book (1975) and *The Waltons Coloring and Activity Book*, Whitman (stock #1254).

CRISSY PAPER DOLLS

Ideal's Crissy and her sister Velvet were popular grow-hair dolls during the late '60s and early '70s. Crissy's distinctive red hair and big brown eyes got her noticed and she became a big seller. Some of the paper dolls related to her, however, seem to be harder to find. For the host of Crissy collectors out there, here are some paper doll sets that you may never had have the chance to see:

Crissy Dress-Up Set, by Colorforms (1970); **Beautiful Crissy Magic Paper Doll,** Whitman #4774, boxed (1971).

Crissy Fashion and Hairstyle Boutique, (left) Whitman (1970); **Crissy Paper Doll with Fun Fashions,** (right) Whitman (1975)

Next to the Crissy and Velvet Coloring Book is the **Crissy and Velvet Paper Doll Set,** both showing a Black Velvet on the cover. Whitman (1970). *(Courtesy of the J. Lawrence Collection.)*

Shirley Temple Paper Doll Masquerade cotumes.

SHIRLEY TEMPLE MASQUERADE COSTUMES

During the height of Shirley Temple's career as a child star, Saalfield produced over twenty paper doll sets in her honor, all big sellers. Today's going prices for these sets are about $60 cut, and about $135 uncut (depending on many factors, including your area of the country). This particular set (the front of which is shown on the left, and the back on the right) is considered the hardest to find, and is valued at about $90 cut, and about $200 uncut.

Inside pages of
**Shirley Temple
Paper Doll
Masquerade
costumes.**

BETSY MCCALL

Betsy McCall, one of the most famous of all paper dolls, was not just on the pages of *McCall* magazine. She also had several paper doll sets through the years that could be purchased at stores. These sets, which are currently very dear to collectors, include:

1. Betsy McCall Fashion Shop (1959) by Standard Toycraft. Original prices were $1.98 for the large set and 98 cents for the small set.

2. Betsy McCall Around the World. Boxed, original price $1.

3. Betsy McCall Dress and Play Paper Dolls, (stock #803) 1959. Boxed, original price $1.

4. Betsy McCall Fashion Designer (1961) Lakeside. Pages to trace and draw. Original price $5.95 (for use with electronic drawing kits).

5. Saalfield Paper Dolls:

   Betsy McCall #5120 (1965). Original price 59 cents.
   Betsy McCall #1360 (1965 & 1966). Original price 29 cents.
   Betsy McCall #4460 (1965 & 1968). Original price 29 cents.
   Betsy McCall #1370 (1965 & 1966). Original price 29 cents.

6. Whitman Paper Dolls

   Betsy McCall #4744 (1971). Boxed, original price $1.29.
   Betsy McCall #1969 (1971). Original price 39 cents.

7. Punch-out set (1971). Boxed; this set came with a coloring book and sold originally for $1.29.

8. A real rarity is the three-foot tall 3-D Paper Sculpture Betsy McCall doll, sold in the November 1954 issue of McCall's magazine. She cost about $1 and came unassembled.

ADDITIONAL PAPER DOLL RARITIES

With the exception of the Liddle Kiddle Doll Box, (bottom, right) the Baby Boom favorites on these pages are not the hardest to find paper doll sets in their series, yet all are considered from hard-to-find to rare when found uncut. The Tammy item is a coloring book—again, hard to find in unused condition.

Baby Boom favorites: **Charmin' Chatty, Skipper Paper Doll, Tutti, and Liddle Kiddles Doll Box.** *(Items courtesy of Terry Carter. Photo courtesy of Patti Cooke.)*

(Items courtesy of Terry Carter. Photos courtesy of Patti Cooke.)

(Items courtesy of Terry Carter. Photos courtesy of Patti Cooke.)

Chatty Baby Stand-up Doll.
*(Item courtesy of Terry Carter.
Photos courtesy of Patti Cooke.)*

Charmin' Chatty Paper Dolls.
(Photos courtesy of Ruth Kibbons.)

Tiny Chatty Twins Paper Dolls.
(Photos courtesy of Ruth Kibbons.)

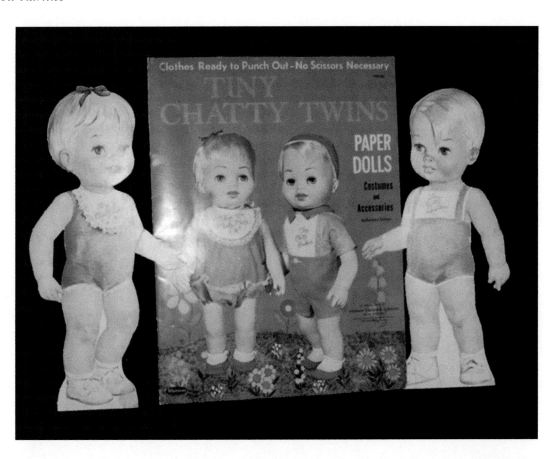

Various **Charmin' Chatty** Paper items.
(Photo courtesy of Ruth Kibbons.)

PAPER DOLL SETS (PAGES 175-176) ARE CONSIDERED HARD TO FIND.

Lennon Sisters
Whitman 1958.
*(Photo courtesy
of Joy Crawford.)*

**Disney's Sleeping Beauty Dolls with
Stay-On Dresses,** Whitman 1958.
(Photo courtesy of Joy Crawford.)

Shirley Temple Snap-On Paper Dolls, Gabriel, #300
(Photo courtesy of Joy Crawford.)

Saalfield **Shirley Temple**
dolls and dresses,
somewhat hard to find
(left); **Dianann Carroll as
Julia paper dolls** (right)
from Artcraft, 1968.
*(Photo courtesy
of Joy Crawford.)*

Elizabeth Taylor dolls (left) and **Gale Storm** dolls (right), both from the 1950s. *(Photo courtesy of Joy Crawford.)*

Mouseketeer cut-outs, Whitman 1957. *(Photo courtesy of Joy Crawford.)*

OTHER RARITIES

THE LUSTRE CREME DOLL

It is difficult to say whether this little platinum blonde with brilliant aqua eyes is hard to find, or if she is simply hiding out anonymously in many a collection. Like the 22-inch Betsy McCall, she is unmarked, but of great interest to those who collect advertising dolls. She could be obtained, originally, as a mail-in premium for Lustre Creme Shampoo. She is an eight-inch hard plastic doll of very good quality, and people who know who she is—perhaps through a childhood memory or an adult interest in either advertising dolls or good quality Ginny-types—have a doozy of a time finding her.

CELLULOID CRAWLING DOLLS

Many of us growing up during the '40s, '50s or '60s can remember with fondness the old familiar neighborhood dime store. An endless supply of plastic or vinyl dolls lined the shelves, with tiny smiling faces and tiny price tags that placed them within our reach. They were the kind of dolls that you didn't have to wait until Christmas for, and that you could play with out in the backyard without upsetting Mom. These "dimestore darlings," as I call them, were, and to some extent still are, plentiful. One of the more rare types is a celluloid crawling doll stamped "Made in Japan" on its feet. Sold in cotton baby rompers, with molded hair and painted features, it had a wind-up mechanism in its stomach that made it crawl. About five to six inches in size, these little guys were either in short supply to begin with, or were too fragile to survive the years, like their hard plastic and vinyl counterparts.

Even more rare is the Black version of this doll, with "curlier" molded hair and very dark skin.

The Lustre Creme Doll.

ORIGINAL BOXES

Another across-the-board hard-to-find doll item is the original box that the doll was packaged in, especially with play dolls. These boxes, which add a considerable amount to a doll's value, are not considered rare, but they definitely present a challenge to the collector. Madame Alexanders, Effanbees, and other dolls that were considered "shelf dolls" are more likely to be found with their original boxes than play dolls such as Kiddles and drink-and-wets.

Shown here is a **Chatty Baby,** by Mattel, with her original box. *(Doll courtesy of Terry Carter. Photo courtesy of Patti Cooke.)*

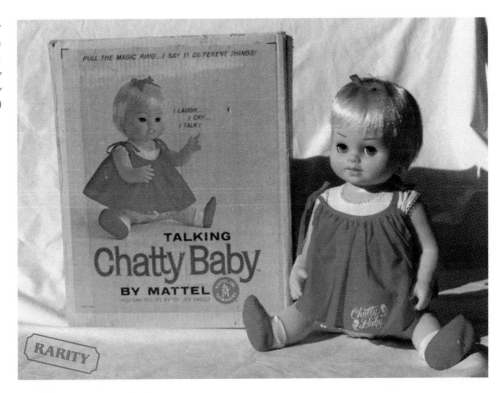

This **Kiddle Kollection** gives collectors an opportunity to see some of the original packaging. Original boxes, packages, cards and hang tags from older dolls are always considered hard to find. *(Items courtesy of Terry Carter. Photos courtesy of Patti Cooke)*

Petite Princess doll house furniture (left) and **Madam Alexander's line of International Dolls** (above). *(Photos courtesy of Lynn Artel and an anonymous Alexander collector.)*

STORE DISPLAYS

Another category of rare items are the original store displays related to today's older collectible dolls. Certain collectors delight at the sight of these displays, as their respective memories came flooding back. We can all remember shopping as a wide-eyed child. And, of course, these displays were specifically made to grab a child's attention. Depicted here is an original store display for Ideal's Petite Princess doll house furniture and for Madam Alexander's line of International Dolls.

VARIOUS RARITIES

Princess Mary, by Ideal, and probably made during the mid-1950s, is a hard-to-find doll that may be of interest to Toni collectors, as she was made with the P-91 Toni body. Her face is distinctly different from Toni's with her stuffed vinyl head and rounded jaw line. With long, straight, dark hair, she is marked "IDEAL DOLL/V91" on her head.

Flatsy Dolls were played with by children who are now in their 30s—the Liddle Kiddle generation. New renditions of these dolls are currently on the market, and the originals, from the 1960s, are starting to take their place among the ranks of respectable collectibles. A Black Flatsy with long combable hair was made during this time frame, and is a very hard-to-find doll. At least one of her original outfits was a polka dot sundress, which may have come in more than one color. Like all original Flatsys, she is completely poseable.

**Fourteen-inch
Linda Williams doll.**
(Photo by the author.)

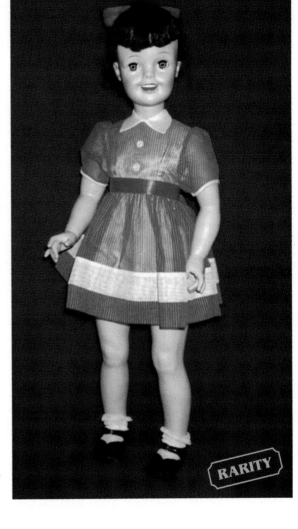

The **30-inch
Linda Williams doll.**
*(Photo courtesy of
John Sonnier.)*

THE 30-INCH
LINDA WILLIAMS DOLL

This brunette ponytailed vinyl doll is marked "LINDA WILLIAMS" on the back of her head, and is meant to be a portrait doll of Angela Cartwright, the child actress who played the character of little Linda on the old hit TV show, "Make Room for Daddy," which starred Danny Thomas, Marjorie Lord and Rusty Hamer. The fourteen-inch version pictured above was a 1959 mail-in premium from General Foods and is rather easy to find. A fifteen-inch variety is also listed in the 1962 Sears Christmas Catalog. Much harder to find is the 30-inch size, probably produced in the same time frame as the very popular Patty Play Pal. Advertisements for this doll showed Angela Cartwright herself, walking hand-in-hand with the doll.

TRESSY RECORD

Made during the 1960s, Tressy was a pioneer among grow-hair dolls. Extremely hard to find is this record album which features a picture of her on the cover, fixing the hair of her little sister, Cricket. Produced by Majorette Records (stock #M-308), the front reads "PLANNING A SHOPPING TRIP, PLAYING BEAUTY PARLOR, GOING TO A PARTY, SONGS, GAMES, FAIRY TALES, FUN!" Most collectors don't even know that it exists!

Tressy Record.
*(Photos courtesy of the
J. Lawrence Collection.)*

ELOISE DOLL

This precious doll was based on a more-than-precocious little girl who was the star of Kay Thompson's 1950s children's books. Living in the Plaza hotel in New York City with her nanny, her dog Weenie, and turtle Skiperdee, Eloise drove the bellhops, chamber maids and hotel detectives crazy—but she did it with great style. Four Eloise books are known to have been printed: *Elosie, Eloise at Christmas, Eloise in Moscow,* and *Eloise in Paris.* I am unsure as to whether there was other related Eloise merchandise. Readers aware of additional Eloise related merchandise are urged to contact the author.

This doll was made in 1958 by Hollytoy Company of New York, and came packaged in a plain cardboard box. She is 23-inches tall, made of cloth, and has a plastic face mask. She is wearing the famous white blouse and black pleated skirt with suspenders, for, even with all of Eloise's wealth, she owned only one outfit for harassing the hotel staff. Today, this doll is very hard to find!

Eloise Doll.
(Photo courtesy of Trisha Nerney.)

Eloise (left);
Eloise in Moscow
(center); and
back cover of
Eloise book (right).
*(Photos by
the Author)*

Talky Crissy. *(Doll courtesy of Tara Wood. Photo courtesy of Paula Carranza.)*

Tara. *(Doll courtesy of Tara Wood. Photo courtesy of Paula Carranza.)*

TALKY CRISSY

Talky Crissy (1971, Ideal) with her pull string in her side, is hard to find. Talky Crissy, with her pull string in her back, is considered rare. Both were part of the Crissy Family of grow-hair dolls. Some of her phrases are: "Let's have a party"; "Hi, I'm Crissy"; and "Make my hair short."

TARA

Another hard-to-find member of the Crissy family of grow-hair dolls is Tara, made in 1970. Shown here with her original outfit and box, she is a stunning doll with unusually dark skin.

MRS. REVLON

We've all heard of Miss Revlon—well, as it turns out, she has a mother who keeps a rather low profile. Here is Mrs. Revlon, the Mother of the Bride. She is a nineteen-inch vinyl doll, with a stuffed one-piece body. She has rooted gray hair, sleep eyes with purple eye shadow, and pierced ears. Made by the Ideal Toy Corporation in 1958, she is marked "14R" on the back of her head, and is very hard to find.

Mrs. Revlon, the Mother of the Bride. *(Photo courtesy of Lynn Barringer Krebs.)*

Additional photos of
Mrs. Revlon. *(Photos courtesy of Lynn Barringer Krebs.)*

LITTLE MARCY

This doll is so rare that few readers of this book will even know who or what she is. Her real value comes from the scattering of people who both remember and love her, and who know what she stood for.

In the middle of the Baby Boom era, children saw films and listened to record albums featuring a fairy-faced little doll named Little Marcy who sang Gospel songs, toned-down for the little ones. With a sparkling personality, a tender voice, and an always-positive message, Little Marcy touched the hearts of children all over the world.

Some examples of her fan mail follows:

"Dear Little Marcy, I am a little girl too. I lost my mother four months ago, and I want to ask you to pray for me. I love your records very much. . ." [Letter from a young girl in Jamaica]

"My sister is writing for me. I am a boy seven years old. I am paralyzed and will never walk. I love your records very much and they help me to spend many happy hours as I lie in bed." [Letter from T.D.]

"Little Marcy, you are so cute. If I had a doll like you I would keep her always in plain site. And I would keep her for my children to see." [Letter from A.D.]

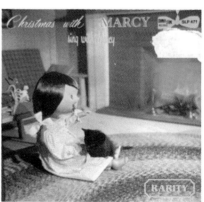

"Christmas with Marcy" album.

"Marcy Sings to Children" album, a **Singcord Recordings advertisement,** and **Marcy & Little Marcy promo photo.**

Little Marcy's creator was Marcy Tigner, a native of Kansas, who provided the voice and vivacity of Little Marcy and encouraged all little children to "listen and be happy with Marcy."

Little fans could write to an Oregon address for a Little Marcy doll of their very own. A tiny point of light, she stands tall in the world of dolls for the heart of the message she tried to impart:

"You'll always be happy, if you walk with the Lord. You'll always be singing if you live by his word."—Little Marcy.

MARTHA THOMPSON'S DOLLS

Martha Thomspon did something unusual—she made porcelain dolls during the 1950s and 60s and in very small numbers. Most of these were sensitive, exacting portraits of celebrities such as Jackie Kennedy, Dwight and Mamie Eisenhower, Grace Kelly, and the British Royal Family. She created four dolls in the image of Prince Charles, depicting him at four different ages (Queen Elizabeth II owns one of the babies). She made small boy and girl dolls, called the McKim Twins, in handknit sweaters—and individual portrait dolls of children and adults, all in very small quantities.

After her first nine designs, Martha, who believed in tithing, designed her tenth doll—"Betsy Sheffield"—and donated these dolls to the Episcopal Church of Sheffield, Alabama for use in fundraising efforts. The ladies of the congregation became "godmothers" for these dolls, sewing outfits for them before they went on sale. Later dolls that followed Betsy in this church fundraising effort were "Betsy's Little Brother" and the "Laughing and Crying Babies." By 1964, total revenues from this project exceeded $15,000—a sizable sum for the 1960s. The clothing made for these dolls by the church ladies is said to provide wonderfully executed examples of handmade doll clothing of the era. The handmade clothing, combined with the beauty of Martha Thompson dolls and the very spirit in which they were given, make these very special and meaningful dolls that are now probably scattered all through Alabama and beyond, with the history of many of them all but forgotten.

Also made were porcelain-head lady dolls including "Little Women" and the Nineteenth Century Group.

The May 1956 issue of *Hobbies* magazine carried an interview with Martha Thompson that provides some insight into the incredible amount of work that went into each of her dolls:

> "I wanted to carry the spirit of each decade in the 19th Century and follow it through the transitions . . . I read everything I could on the subject . . . By trying different materials for the decorations, I finally arrived at a satisfactory method . . . For my short hair . . . I began with moderately fine crochet cotton and cut the strands into short lengths, arranged it on the head; piece by piece, and painted it down with a paint brush and clay slip, building up the dolls as I went . . . For making curls I use a very thin steel sock knitting needle, the smallest made . . . As soon as the curl has dried out enough not to be sticky, it is slipped off the needle in a long snake curl and "canned" in a glass cigar case with others, tightly corked to keep it damp until I can cut it into the proper lengths to attach to the doll head. Everything has to be kept damp and I frequently keep a head which is being worked on under a glass dome with a wet sponge enclosed until I can work on it some more. I use different sizes of cotton string for different effects . . . flowers are made of clay which has been mixed with glycerin to keep pliable, rolled out like dough and cut, petal by petal . . . it is painstaking work and there are many interruptions . . ."

In a toy magazine, she wrote: "*I won't dwell on it again . . . it's a nightmare . . . but when it is finally done right, it is such a satisfaction.*"

Martha Thompson was born in Huntsville, Alabama in the early 1900s and she died in January of 1964. Owners of one or more of her rare and beautiful dolls are asked to contact the author.

THE SIDE-PART BETSY McCALL

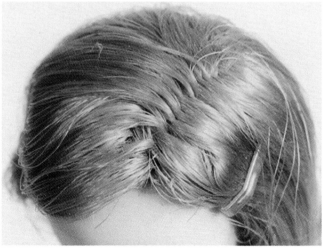

Photos of the extremely rare side-part, eight-inch, hard plastic **Betsy McCall doll.** This example is in mint condition. *(Photos courtesy of Tina Ritari.)*

BETSY MCCALL DESIGNER STUDIO

An incredible find, Mint in Box, is this darling and imaginative set that includes fabric, lace, thread, pin and a dressmaker's form to help create eight-inch Tiny Betsy McCall's "instant wardrobe."

Other rare gift sets for Tiny (eight-inch) Betsy McCall are: At the Ranch (one doll, three outfits); A Day with Betsy (one doll, three outfits); Beach Party (one doll, outfit, towel, umbrellas, and sailboat); and Garden Party (one doll, one outfit, flower pot, shovel and real seeds).

Other hard-to-find Betsy McCall items are:

1. **Betsy McCall Treasure Trunk:** A cardboard trunk meant to hold the paper dolls cut out from *McCall's* magazine, it came with three pastel handkerchiefs. Sold originally for $1.

2. **Betsy McCall Storybooks:** Complete with paper dolls, sold in late 1950s to early '60s. Publishers were Little Golden Books and Golden Press. Original price was $1.

3. **Betsy McCall Travel Pack:** Complete with cosmetics which included lipstick, talc, toilet water and more, the kit came in a black patent leather zip-case with a handle. Also included was a booklet on beauty tips and a travel diary. Original price was $3.95.

4. **Betsy McCall Sing Along Party Album:** Advertised in magazines in 1963 and 1964 and then again in 1969, this $33^1/_3$-rpm record offered over 35 songs and a sing-a-long book. Original price was $2.98. Also available was a 45- and 78-rpm record sung by Rosemary Clooney called "Betsy, My Paper Doll." Original price was $1.40.

5. **Betsy McCall Pretty Pac:** Made by HMSCO in the late 1950s, this was a round zip-case with a soft handle that came in more than one variation—all with cosmetics, some with an umbrella. Original prices range from $3.33 to $6.00.

6. **Betsy McCall Dishes and Silverware:** A set for girls with Betsy's picture and a set for boys with Jimmy Week's (Betsy's friend) picture. Nine-inch round plates with extended sides held the silverware: a fork and a spoon.

22-inch Betsy McCall

This doll is not considered particularly rare, but deserves some mention as she is continually passed up by general collectors. She is a 22-inch Betsy McCall, and she is unmarked. Besides this picture, an easy way to identify her is the fact that she is multi-jointed. Her neck, shoulders, wrists, waist and ankles are all jointed; and her thighs are jointed twice.

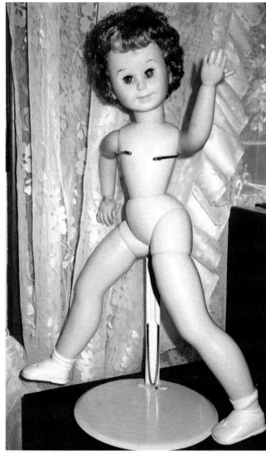

Two pictures of the
22-inch Betty McCall doll.
(Photos by the author.)

36-inch Shirley Temple dolls. *(Photo courtesy of John Sonnier.)*

Honey-Blonde Tiny Tears (left);
Brunette Tiny Tears (right.)

36-INCH SHIRLEY TEMPLE DOLLS

SO-O-O hard to find and such a real treat to gaze upon are these mint 36-inch Shirley Temple dolls. Thank you, John Sonnier, for sharing them with us!!

BRUNETTE TINY TEARS

The vinyl American Character Tiny Tears from the early '60s was a very popular baby doll in her day. She was one of the front runners in the "Diaper Derby" of that era, when drink-and-wet dolls were very much in demand. Her head was of hard plastic with her tight curls rooted into a softer skull cap. She was pleasingly chubby, and yet had a distinct daintiness about her, with her tiny twinkling eyes and her pin-dot of a nurser mouth, which is drawn up like a bow. Very appealing then and now, she is a favorite with collectors. The great majority of these dolls were a dark honey blonde. Harder to find is the brunette version.

GINNY RARITIES

1. **Porcelain Ginny:** In 1990, a beautiful brown-eyed brunette porcelain Ginny was made. She had a head and shoulder plate and arms and legs, all made of porcelain, and a cloth stuffed body, in the style of an antique doll. Only 1,000 of these dolls were said to have been made, and they are, unfortunately, unmarked. This porcelain Ginny is not to be confused with the porcelain Ginnys made and sold during the mid-80s, which were all porcelain and marked "GINNY/ c VOGUE DOLLS/INC/" on their backs. At least one of her outfits was a reproduction of a the 1954 "Bridesmaid" outfit (stock #54).

2. **Black Ginny:** Very rare is the Black Ginny, produced during the years 1953 and 1954. She had beautiful coloring, with light brown skin and deep rose cheek blush. She came as either a walker or a non-walker, and with either short, soft curls or with braids—both with dark brown hair.

3. **Ginny Storybook Lamps:** True treasures to fall upon are the Ginny Storybook Lamps, manufactured in the 1940s. Each lamp featured a Ginny Doll, dressed up as either Little Bo Peep, Little Red Riding Hood, or Toddles, which could be unclipped from the base of the lamp to be played with. This, no doubt, explains why few of them are found intact. The lamps were fourteen-inches high, with a simple wooden square for Ginny to stand on as the base, and frilly fabric lamp shades to match the doll's dress. These lamps sold originally for about $5.

4. **Commemorative Doll:** In 1986, the Modern Doll Convention used Ginny for their annual Commemorative Doll. Limited to a very exclusive issue of only 75, she was painted by Jamie Englert and is in a gown of beautiful tea rose pink, with a cranberry cape—both of slipper satin. She carries a presentation bouquet and wears a sequined crown.

5. **Meyer's Specials:** These are also Ginnys that were limited in production, and are now sought after by newer Ginny collectors who are just learning of their existence. The costuming on these dolls, especially the first two years, is dazzling.

   1986 Fairy Godmother: In a pale china blue gown and "hennin" (cone-shaped princess hat), with rich gold lace and trim and embroidered floral appliqués, she was limited to only 500.

   1987 Cinderella and Prince Charming: As with the 1986 Fairy Godmother, designer Ann Cottrell, took pains to create some historically authentic costumes. Prince Charming is in a striking Elizabethan-style jacket and breeches, with a flood of ruffles at the collar and cuffs. Cinderella is in an English rose-colored high-waist gown, with a gold lace overdress, generously accented with gold braid, ruffled lace and satin bows. This elegant couple was limited to a production of 1,000.

   1988 Clown: A curly-topped redhead in full clown makeup and a frosty pink and lilac clown suit with accessories. He (?) was limited to a production of 1,000.

6. **Ginny Paper Products:** This includes paper plates, cups, napkins and tablecloths meant for children's birthday parties. One known set was called "Party Papers" by the Gibson Company, and featured drawings of both Ginny and Ginnette. They are extremely rare.

7. **Ginny Christmas Items:** These include cards sent out during the 1950s to Ginny owners from the company; and Ginny Christmas Stockings made of a net material with a paper top labeled "GINNY" and filled with goodies. Like any paper or otherwise disposable product, few of these items have survived the years, but writing about them may help to uncover a few more.

OTHER GINNY RARITIES

All of Ginny's Trunk Sets and Gift Sets from the 1950s are difficult to find, especially intact, but are well worth the hunt, as they are beautiful representations of a bygone era. One particularly rare gift set, made in 1956, is Ginny's Party Package

Unidentified **Ginny Outfit**.
(Photo courtesy of Jackie Litchfield.)

A rare transitional **Ginny** from 1951 with violet eyes. *(Photo courtesy of O'Connell/Schoenick.)*

(stock #6859). It included a Dress Me Ginny, surrounded by extra clothing and accessories that included a straw hat, slippers and a hand mirror. There were at least two variations of this gift set.

Sparky, Ginny's tiny Fox Terrier made by Steiff during the 1950s, is hard to find, especially with his plaid dog coat.

UNIDENTIFIED GINNY OUTFIT

Here is a Ginny outfit that collectors can't seem to identify. It has the "VOGUE DOLLS INC/MEDFORD, MASS, USA/*REG US PAT OFF" tag, which would put it in the 1954-56 time frame. The doll wearing the outfit is a molded-lash Ginny, which also fits into this time frame. The cotton bodice is a short sleeved floral print with a hook-and-eye closure, and the skirt is of a light pink organdy with gold braid trim. There are also pink organdy bloomers and a straw hat trimmed with the same pink organdy and gold braid trim.

Here is a very rare Ginny article owned by Joyce O'Connell—a Ginny Caracul wig, from about 1952, with its own case and the glue that came with it. The outside of the canister reads "Hi, I'm Ginny . . . I'll be just as good as new when you replace my hairdo."

Top: **Ginny Caracul wig.** Left: Rare doll soap made by **Vogue** in the early 1950s. *(Photos courtesy of O'Connell/Schoenick.)*

Suzy Cute Rarities

Interest in all Ginnette-size baby dolls from the Baby Boom era is starting to climb. These tiny babies have a charm and enchantment all their own. Children love them and adults recognize how engaging they can be when set up on a shelf with all of their fixtures and furnishings—a miniaturized panorama of one of life's great joys, a new baby.

Even people who did not have Suzy Cute as children fall in love with her when they first see her. With a face that is the essence of "cute," the doll herself is somewhat scarce, and her play sets and outfits are hard to find.

Suzy Cute's Outfits

Suzy Cute's boxed outfits were darling, and similar in style to the Ginnette outfits from the 1950s, but not as elaborate. The photo on the left shows Honey 'N Spice (yellow and embroidered with hens and chicks), Winter Angel (red snow set with white fur trim), and Sweet Dreams (pink PJs with embroidered lollipop). The picture at right shows Hop Skip 'N Jump (blue and white sun set with an embroidered duck family), Splash 'N Dry (white terry robe with diaper and accessories), and Fancy Frills, a favorite with collectors, (powder blue party dress with floral embroidery).

All of Suzy Cute's Play sets are presently considered hard-to-find to rare. Suzy Cute collectors are not as networked as Barbie or Chatty collectors, for example, so it is difficult to determine whether these items are as scarce as they seem to be, or if some of them could be laying around attics and basements unidentified. Shown on the following page are her Swing Set, Stroller, Feeding Chair, Dresser, Carriage, and Bathinette, all easily identified by those distinctive round plastic medallions that are an earmark of Suzy Cute items.

Suzy Cute's Pamphlet showing **"Honey 'N Spice," "Winter Angel," "Sweet Dreams", "Hop Skip 'N Jump," "Splash 'N Dry,"** and **"Fancy Frills"**

FEEDING CHAIR

Mealtime fun in Suzy Cute's **FEEDING CHAIR** . . . just like a real baby. She has her own DISH, SPOON, CUP and BIB. Set includes handy HASSOCK and pet PLASTIC PUPPY to keep her company. Made of strong plastic with decorative colored animal buttons.

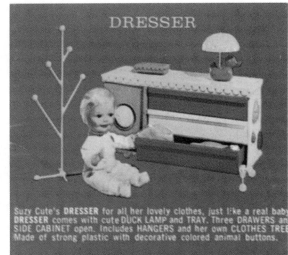

DRESSER

Suzy Cute's **DRESSER** for all her lovely clothes, just like a real baby. DRESSER comes with cute DUCK LAMP and TRAY. Three DRAWERS and SIDE CABINET open. Includes HANGERS and her own CLOTHES TREE. Made of strong plastic with decorative colored animal buttons.

CARRIAGE

Take her everywhere in Suzy Cute's **CARRIAGE**. Just like a real baby, CARRIAGE has a MOVEABLE HOOD. Includes her very own BOTTLE. Made of strong plastic with decorative colored animal buttons.

BATHINETTE

Time for Suzy Cute's bath. Just like a real baby, Suzy's **BATHINETTE** really holds water. Includes PLAY BOTTLES and TERRY TOWEL, DUCK and FISH water toys. Made of strong plastic with decorative colored animal buttons.

SWING SET

Time for play, just like a real baby — Suzy slides, glides and swings in her **SWING SET**. Includes her own plastic PAIL, SHOVEL and red and yellow bouncing BALL. Made of strong plastic with decorative colored animal buttons.

STROLLER

Take her walking . . . just like a real baby's, Suzy Cute's **STROLLER** has a SUNSHADE that moves up and down and TRAY to carry her toys. Includes RATTLE and PLASTIC ANIMAL. Made of strong plastic with decorative colored animal buttons.

(Clockwise from left): **Feeding Chair, Dresser, Carriage, Bathinette, Swing Set,** and **Stroller.**

RARITY

PENNY BRITE RARITIES

In 1963, the Deluxe Reading Toy Company offered American little girls a delightful alternative to Barbie. Penny Brite, an eight-inch vinyl darling with light, copper-colored hair, had an array of out-

fits, accessories and playsets just as Barbie did, but was fashioned as a little girl rather than a teenager, giving young girls the opportunity to relate to her and act out events that occur in their everyday lives.

Her collection of outfits included the types of clothing that young girls could wear to school, Sunday school, a day at the beach or an afternoon at the skating rink. There was even an ensemble named "Flower Girl," every little girl's dream. She came in a pleated red and white cotton A-line style dress with a crisp white collar and tiny flower appliqués. All outfits were well made and attentively accessorized.

Cute as a button,
bright as a Penny . . .

Her playsets were, unfortunately, not quite as well made as her clothing, and it seems as though fewer of them survived the years to make appearances on today's collector's market. There has been a rising interest in these playsets among collectors, as their relative scarcity is slowly being acknowledged.

Her Bedroom Set was constructed of yellow molded plastic and the bedding was of orange cotton trimmed in white lace. The set included a canopy bed, skirted vanity and bench, two lamps and her own pair of PJs. The quality of lace used and its method of gathering is somewhat disappointing.

The Kitchen Dinette Set followed the same orange and yellow color scheme in molded plastic. The set included a kitchen cabinet and sink, a dinette set, and such added extras as a miniature set of dishes and glasses and a dish drainer; pots, pans and a Lazy Susan; and a dress and apron set for Penny.

The School Room Set contained a plastic school desk and a blackboard on an easel. It also included a chalk and eraser for the child, and a school bag, book and pen for Penny. The set came with a checked jumper for Penny that was a dead ringer for the Catholic grade school uniform that I wore in 1963. I don't remember looking anywhere near that cute in my uniform—I guess that Penny was just small enough to pull it off.

Her Beauty Parlor Set came with a chair, hair dryer, sink, mirror, and a smock for Penny to wear.

And finally, the Travel Set offered a plastic convertible-style car, a hat and coat for Penny, and her own set of luggage.

As you can see by the descriptions, Deluxe Reading is to be commended for the special fuss they exerted in including so many special extras, and giving the children who played with Penny that much more to delight in.

Even though her face was probably an imitation of Ideal's Tammy, in her time Penny Brite became popular enough to have a few knock-offs of her own. Apple-cheeked dolls with side-glancing eyes were produced by other companies under such names as "Little Tuppence" and "Posing Penny" in an effort to capitalize on Deluxe Reading's little gold mine!

Penny Brite's original
outfits: *"Chit Chat,"*
"Singing in the Rain,"
"Sun and Fun,"
"Winter Princess,"
"Anchors Aweigh,"
and *"Flower Girl."*
(Photo by author.)

As more and more Baby Boomers catch the wave of nostalgia, Penny Brite becomes more and more collectible. She must have had just the right amount of appeal at just the right price, because it seems that there was at least one or two on every block. Being inexpensive makes a doll more accessible on the one hand, and more disposable on the other. Quite a few of these little dolls were likely discarded over the years. At present, Penny herself is not very hard to find, but her many playsets and boxed outfits are hard to find, especially intact. If you are among those with a rising interest in this doll, the following are a few things that you may not have seen for some 30 years, or may never have seen at all!

The Penny Brite Kitchen Dinette Set had lots of small details, including working cabinet doors (both hinged and sliding), a draining basket with real miniature dishes, a lazy susan, and a Penny Brite paper doll wearing a cotton dress and apron that could be placed on a real Penny Brite doll!

Penny Brite's Beauty Parlor Set included a manicure table with tiny bottles of polish, a mirrored sink that could hold water, a pivoting, very "sixties" hood hair dryer and beauty shop chair, and the paper doll wore a yellow and blue smock. (Look for the "P" on the smock—it makes it easy to identify at flea markets.) Her Bedroom Set had a four-poster canopy bed with bed linens, a skirted vanity table with two lamps, and blue pajamas that came in two versions, with either checked or solid white trim.

Anyone who attended Saint Lambert's Grade School in Skokie, Illinois during the 1960s, will recognize the outfit that Penny is wearing in her School Room Set—either evoking blissful memories or sending shivers down the spine. The set also included a real chalk board, tiny school supplies, and a Penny-sized briefcase. Her Travel Set was a blue convertible with bucket seats and a luggage rack, so Penny could motor down the scenic highways of "Dollyland," the only place on earth that allows a six-year-old to obtain a driver's license. The white dog included in the set is particularly hard to find.

Penny Brite's little sister, Baby Brite, is more difficult to find than Penny. She may not have been as popular as Penny and perhaps fewer were made to begin with. She was not done in the eight-inch format like Penny. At 13^1/$_2$ inches, she is closer to the size of a standard baby doll. Her white Baby Brite Nursery is a charming set with molded baby animals and cute detail and is now hard to find.

SCHOOL ROOM

SCHOOLROOM—Penny Brite learns her ABC's like a real little girl. • Desk and Chair—modern as today's newest schoolroom. • Blackboard and Easel is a real one with chalk and eraser. • Brushes realistically designed... there's also a pen and book. • Includes simulated Penny Brite Doll* wearing actual Penny Brite 2-piece schoolgirl dress. *Penny Brite Doll is sold separately in her combination wardrobe-carrying case.

BEDROOM SET

BEDROOM—There are 3 gracefully designed pieces of furniture. • Bed with canopy, bedspread and pillow. • Dresser Unit with ruffled skirt—mirror and 2 lamps. • Stool • Two Piece Pajama Set. Includes simulated Penny Brite Doll* wearing 2-piece pajama. What girl won't want to say, "Good-Night" to Penny Brite with this play set? *The Penny Brite Doll is sold separately in her combination wardrobe-carrying case.

KITCHEN DINETTE

KITCHEN-DINETTE is as real as life. • Sink Cabinet. Sink has a sliding door with dishes. Sink has a door and removable drip pan. Rinse tray contains saucers. • Dinette Table and Chairs... table has lazy susan and glasses. Set includes simulated Penny Brite Doll* wearing 2-piece dress and apron. *Penny Brite Doll sold separately in her combination wardrobe-carrying case.

BEAUTY PARLOR

BEAUTY PARLOR—Penny Brite is a pretty girl and little girls can keep her pretty with this Beauty Parlor. • Hair Dryer has padding bond. • Beauty Parlor Chair turns and tilts. • Sink and Stool. Sink has mirror and holds water so you can wash Penny Brite's hair. • Complete with simulated Penny Brite Doll* wearing attractive Beauty Parlor Smock. *The Penny Brite Doll is sold separately in her combination wardrobe-carrying case.

Complete set fully assembled—ready for play in this beautifully illustrated take-home package.

TRAVEL SET

TRAVEL SET—Penny Brite is a doll who travels in style. • Sports Car—with luxuriously styled bucket-seat cushions, glamorous dashboard, metallized luggage rack, hub caps, radio antenna. • Luggage—suitcase, hatbox and shoulder bag to match. • Pet Dog. Includes simulated Penny Brite Doll* wearing actual Penny Brite coat and hat. *Penny Brite Doll is sold separately in her combination wardrobe-carrying case.

Penny Brite sets (clockwise from left): "School Room"; "Bedroom Set"; "Kitchen Dinette"; and "Beauty Parlor." *(All photos are from the original Penny Brite brochure and were taken by author.)*

RARITY

BABY BRITE NURSERY—This amazing new baby doll is 13½" tall, with rooted hair, and wearing a cuddly pink pajama. Baby Brite's Nursery has everything a "Little Mother" needs. (All decorated with molded animal figures.) Baby Tender—can be converted to flat table top, has feeding dish, spoon. Bathinette—Complete with towel, sponge, drain pan. Crib—Has pink Box Mattress.

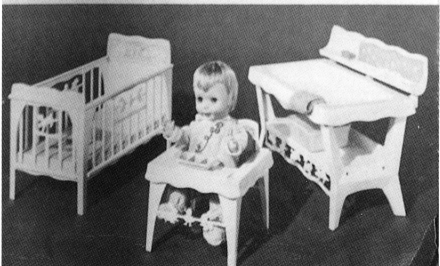

Push the magic button when Baby Brite is lying down.... Baby Brite turns her head, closes her eyes and goes to sleep.

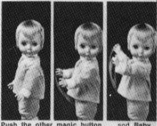

Push the other magic button.... and Baby Brite raises her arms to be picked up.

Baby Brite Nursery, (left) **Baby Brite,** (right) Penny Brite's little sister.

INDEX

Alexander Co. 111-113
    Patty 113
    rarities 113
Alexanderkins 111-112
    hard-to-find 112, 112
    rare 112
Baby Teenietalk 120
Barbie .1-19
    American Girl . . . . .x, 2, 6, 7, 13
    Boudoir Clock 18
    Bubble Cut 1, 4, 9, 10
    Cinnamon American Girl 13
    Color Magic 2
    Comic Books 15
    Current Hard-to-Find 19
    Costume Trunk 16
    Dressed display dolls 4
    Fashion Queen 1
    Genuine Mink 15
    Greeting Cards 16
    Hair Happenin's 14
    International Market dolls . . .11, 12
    Kokusai Boeki House 17
    Living Barbie 18
    Miss Barbie 2
    outfits 12, 13
    Photo Clock 18
    Play Ring 14
    Ponytail 1, 3, 4, 18
    Record album 14
    Redhead Twist & Turn 13
    Shops by Phone Set 17
    Side-part American Girl . . . . . .vi, 5
    Side-part Bubble Cut 7
    Stationary 16
    Swirl 2, 8, 9
    Trade-in 14
    Transistor Radio 10
    Travel Trunk 17
    Twist 'N Turn (Twist & Turn) . . .2, 10
    Vanity Case 26
    Wedding Party Gift Set 26

Betsy McCall 161- 162, 171-172,
                       185-187
    22-inch unmarked 187
    Designer Studio 186
    other rarities 186, 187
    side part 185
Cabbage Patch 80-89
    "A" dolls 82
    "B" dolls 82
    "C" dolls 82, 87
    "D" dolls 82
    "E" dolls 83
    1980 Celebrity dolls 83
    1980 Grand Edition 83
    1980 Special Preemie 83
    Helen Blue 80, 82, 86, 87
    Little People Pals 89
    Nicholas and Noel 83
    rare Coleco 83-85, 88-89
    "U" dolls 83
    various types 81
    "X" Christmas dolls 82
Cathy Quickcurl 120
Celluloid crawling dolls 177
Chatty Cathy 27-41
    Amber-eyed 37
    Black 30-32
    Blue and White Jumper 37
    Brown-eyed Blonde 29
    clothing v
    hair color variations 33, 34
    Hard-face Pageboy 40
    Nursery Set 40, 41
    Olive-eyed 30
    original packaging 178
    paper dolls 168, 173-174
    Pencil Post Bed 38
    Playtable 41
    rooting variation 36
    Soft-face Pigtail 39-40
    Strawberry Blonde 34-35
    TV Tray 38

various types 28-29
    with Charmin' Hair 32
Crissy Family 169-170, 182
Dawn 135-139
    Country Place 138
    gas station promotions 137
    Green-eyed Dale 137
    Head to Toe dolls 138
    Jewelry Boxes 139
    Lunchboxes 137
    Pageant Cape 138
    rare outfits 137, 138
    store displays 139
    Umbrella 138
    various types 135-136
Doll Buggies 151-154
    19th century 152
    20th century 152
    Chatty Cathy 153, 154
    Shirley Temple 153
Effanbee Co. 140-142
    limited editions 141-142
    other rarities 142
    various dolls 141
Eloise doll 181
Francie 20-22
    Black 22
    Japanese 22
    No Bangs 20, 21
    various types 21
Ginnette 71-75
    Black 73
    chest of drawers 75
    Jimmy Clown 74
    Jimmy Cowboy 74
    red shoes 74
Ginny 188-190
    Black 188
    Christmas items 189
    Commemorative doll 189
    other rare items 189, 190
    paper products 189

porcelain 188
Store specials 189
Storybook lamps 189
Horseman Co. 148-150
rare dolls 150
various dolls 149
Jem 143-147
2nd issue Shanna and Ava 146
hard-to-find fashions 147
Mail-in Premiums 146
story of 143-145
various types 145
Jill .76-79
Brown-eyed 76, 77
dressed doll in box 78-79
Flip-Hair variation 78
other rare items 79
Ken 16, 18
Liddle Kiddles 42-58
3-D Postcard 58
Alice in Wonderliddle's Castle . . .57
Baby Liddle 56
Beat-A-Diddle 53
Cinderiddle's Palace 56
Coloring Books 54
Electric Drawing Desk 58
Frame Tray Puzzles 58
hairstyle variations 58
Jewelry Treasure Box 52
Lunchbox and Thermos Kit 52
Magic Slate 56
original packaging 178
paper dolls 169, 172
Play Fun Set 55
record album 51
related collectibles 49-51
Rolly Twiddle 54
Spanish Sticker Book 52
Sticker Pictures 55
Town 55
Trade and Color Set 58
Treasure Trio 55
various types 43-48
wallet 58
Zoolery Kiddles 57
Linda Williams doll 180
Little Marcy 183-184
Lustre Creme doll 177
Marth Thompson's dolls 184-185
Mattel Co. 114-120
common dolls ('60s & '70s) . .115-117
other rarities 118
Midge 18
Casey 18

No Freckles 17
Wig Wardrobe 18
Mrs. Revlon 182-183
original packaging 178
Paper Dolls 155-176
1920s and 1930s 158
1940s 159
Baby Boom era 159-161
collecting hints 162
Crissy 169-170
current 162
early 1800s 156
Gilded Age 157
mid 1800s 156
other rarities 172-176
Shirley Temple 170-171, 175
turn of the century 157
values 164-166
Waltons, The 169
Penny Brite 193-195
Baby Brite 195
outfits 193, 194
play sets 193-194, 195
Robert, Xavier 81, 82, 86
Sasha 106-110
Harlequin 109
Kiltie 109
Pintucks 109
Prince Gregor 110
Princess 110
Sari 110
various types 108
Velvet 109
Shirley Temple, 36 inch 188
Singin' Chatty, green-eyed 118
Skipper 23-26
1970 Reissue 26
1970 Trade-in 26
Blonde Pose & Play 26
Bunk Beds 26
Japanese 26
rare outfits 26
Skipper On Wheels Gift Set 26
Swing-A-Rounder Gym 26
Vanity Case 26
various types 23-25
store displays 139, 179
Storybook Small Talks 119
Suzy Cute 191-192
outfits 191
play sets 192
Tammy 91-105
Black 96

Brunette Mom 98
Brunette Straight Leg 99
Bud .94
car .101
Carrot Top Pepper 96, 97
Catamaran 100
furniture 101
hair dryer case 94
hard-to-find cases 102-103
hard-to-find outfits 103-105
Juke Box 100
Lunchboxes 99, 100
paper dolls 167, 173
Patti .95
pencil case 101
Pete and Salty 98
purse 94
record albums 93
various types 91
Terri Lee 59-70
Alice in Wonderland 65
Black 63-64
Composition 64
Ferris Wheel 62
Gene Autry doll 66
Hispanic 64
lamps 70
other rare items 70
paper dolls 167
Pig-tailed 69
Snobby Poodle 69
Steiff monkeys 68
Talking . . . . .vi, 67
various types 59-61
vinyl .66
Walker 68
wardrobe cabinets 70
Tiny Tears, brunette 188
Tressy record 181
Trolls 121-133
Black 127
Brides 126
Denmark 123-125
English 125-126
Houses 130-131
other rarities 131-133
packaged 128-129
Pixie 128
Santas 126
Superheroes 127
Trollettes 128
Valerie 120

ABOUT THE AUTHOR

Author at age 6
with Chatty Cathy.

Carla Marie Cross, born Carla Marubio, grew up in Suburban Chicago and never met a doll she didn't like. her childhood favorites were Barbie, Tiny Tears, Wendy Ann Alexanderkin and Thumbelina.

A former teacher and day care administrator, she had her own line of children's clothing, Little Bo Buttons. Today, married with four children, she has authored over 100 articles on dolls and collectible toys, and is an avid collector of modern dolls as well as older children's books, china and crystal.

In addition to writing and collecting, she photographs dolls for various magazines, is active in charitable fundraising, and loves heirloom sewing, cross stitch, silk ribbon embroidery, crochet and sketching portraits.

MODERN DOLL
Rarities

Carla Marie Cross

ATB